BEST OF THE BEST PRESENTS

LOW-CARB ESSENTIALS
EVERYDAY LOW-CARB RECIPES YOU'LL LOVE TO COOK
and eat!

GEORGE STELLA
WITH **CHRISTIAN STELLA**

Q QUAIL RIDGE PRESS

Published by
QUAIL RIDGE PRESS
www.quailridge.com

Library of Congress Control Number: 2015957402

First printing, January 2016 • Second, February 2016

Authors:
George Stella
with Christian Stella

Book Design and Interior Food Photography by
Christian and Elise Stella

This book is not meant to dispense medical advice. Please consult your doctor before making any dramatic changes to the way you eat.

Nutritional analysis provided on each recipe is meant only as a reference and has been compiled to the best of our ability using nutritional analysis software. Due to differences in sizes, brands, and types of ingredients, your calculations may vary. Calories have been rounded to the nearest 5 and all other amounts were rounded to the nearest .5 of a gram.

ISBN 978-1-938879-17-3
Manufactured in the United States of America
by CJK Print Possibilities • Cincinnati, Ohio

CONTENTS

INTRODUCTION

AN ESSENTIAL CHANGE

Fifteen years ago, the scene around the Stella family dinner table looked bleak. There was usually a stack of pizza boxes. Empty soda cans and bottles were thrown into a recycling bin between our feet. Then there was us...all twelve hundred-plus pounds of us.

My wife Rachel found herself at over two hundred pounds. My son Anthony, pushing 230, bordered on obese. My younger son Christian was *already* obese at the age of fifteen, weighing over 300 pounds. Wheeling around my kitchen in this great big captain's chair I salvaged from the side of the road, I sat more comfortably than when I used my actual wheelchair—but I was hardly comfortable—it's hard to ever be comfortable at 467 pounds.

I had become familiar with the emergency room by then. I'd been struck by my first heart attack way, way back when I was young and athletic, but now morbidly obese, I was the definition of risk to have another. I was falling apart. A third bout of pneumonia in little over a year's time put me back into the hospital. That was what spurred a doctor to finally spell it out for me. He so frankly told me, "George, you are going to die."

There I was, bound to my captain's chair at the helm of my own version of a sinking ship. I was on disability, with congestive heart failure and a future full of sleep apnea-ruined nights. The doctor was right. My eating was killing me—but even worse—I had an entire family following in my footsteps. With such a large problem on my plate, it seemed next to impossible to pinpoint a solution. I knew what *had* to be done.

I just had no idea where to *begin*.

I've told this story so many times and always thought it important to mention the copy of *Dr. Atkins New Diet Revolution* someone left behind at our house all those years ago. If Rachel had not read the entire book cover to cover and convinced the rest of us that this was not only doable, but worth a try, well, I don't know where we would be today. We certainly wouldn't have had the courage to change our lives the way we did. Low-carb seemed too simple. So simple, it was silly. It was the total opposite of what we thought we needed to do in order to lose the weight.

But, what else—besides weight—did I have to lose? Looking back now, I realize I had a lot more to gain than I ever lost. I was on a path to gaining my life back.

I am a firm believer that if you want to lose weight, if you are really ready to lose weight, you absolutely can. Regardless of what you call the way you eat, you can lose weight by eating fresh, healthy food. My family doesn't give full credit for our weight loss to The Atkins Diet, or any other diet for that matter, because we never followed any one particular plan from beginning to end. We learned the *essentials* and carved out our own path after that. We learned about food and changed our habits. But we didn't *diet*. Diet plans are rigid, repetitive, and hardly what you'd call "fun." They breed boredom, and boredom feeds bad habits.

As someone who was once 467 pounds, I think I can say with conviction that eating is a big part of life. Not just in that it sustains life, but that a lot of life revolves around eating. During a lot of life's best moments—holidays, dates, even a night at the movies—food is there. We all *love* to eat, and there's nothing wrong with that. What we *need* to love more is…cooking.

When you find true joy in cooking—when you find that preparing a home-cooked meal is genuinely fun—that's when you find success. That's when you start filling your grocery carts with real food, not packaged junk, and things really change.

Things truly changed for us! The four of us lost over 560 pounds together as a family and have never looked back. Rachel and Anthony each dropped over 70 pounds. Christian lost more than half his body weight, going from 305 to under 150, and I did away with the 265 pounds that would have surely been the death of me. These weren't instant transformations, but as close to instant as I could imagine. I was slowly dying as I ate pizza at the dining room table…. Then two years later I was back where I belonged, working as a professional chef in a five-star restaurant.

Almost as soon as we lost the weight, our story started to spread. Within that same year, multiple magazines ran articles on us, countless television producers were calling to do interviews…. I even wrote my first cookbook. Most notably, I had landed my own show on the Food Network, *Low Carb and Lovin' It*. Though it only aired for two seasons, the fans we gained from the show's running stuck around through the years and continue to follow us to this day. Their own stories of success never cease to amaze us. I've told our family's story so many times, but there's always someone new to hear it. Someone that can create their own success story. Just maybe that is you?

Arugula Pesto Chicken, *page 99*

THE ESSENTIALS OF LOW-CARB

As a chef, I spend my time in the kitchen. I am not a doctor or nutritionist, just someone who can cook a pretty mean steak and someone who has over fifteen years experience cooking and eating low carb.

I will do my best to summarize how low-carb works, but just know that I am not the author to explain *why* it works. The specifics of what occurs inside the body would be better left for a doctor to describe. Dr. Atkins and other doctors wrote entire 500-page books exploring the subject. There are also countless studies available on the Internet that also clarify the effectiveness of low carb.

The concept of eating low carb is actually quite simple to explain. Our bodies are capable of converting either carbohydrates or fat into the energy needed to function, however, our bodies also prefer carbohydrates when they are available. Eating a diet full of carbohydrates causes the body to burn only the carbs necessary to get through the day before then converting the remaining carbohydrates into fat, which is then stored in the event there ever comes a time when excess fat is needed for survival. This is the reason that overeating leads to weight gain—in this way, we are similar to bears storing fat for hibernation in the winter.

Your body can also create energy from fat when not supplied with an ample amount of carbohydrates. By converting fat into energy, your body goes into a constant fat-burning state known as "ketosis." Not only do you burn the fat that you eat, you always burn up the reserves meant to get you through the day. Most people find it hard to grasp why low carb allows you to eat fattier foods. There's a simple explanation—your body burns it right off.

Entering the "ketosis" state is easily achieved; simply stop eating processed carbohydrates. It's staying in a state of "ketosis" that is most important to success. Cheating on a low-carb lifestyle immediately switches your body out of "ketosis" and back to burning carbohydrates and *storing* fat.

Studies have proven time and again that low carb actually works, when on "ketosis," and my family is a testament that it can work long term. Once committed, you've got to commit in order to see results.

Low carb, for us, was ultimately just a lifestyle switch, a decision to bypass processed, packaged foods generally considered unhealthy, and instead stick with only fresh ingredients found in the outer aisles of the grocery store. Almost as *essential* to our success as choosing the right foods, we also decided to get back into the kitchen and cook for ourselves, taking pride in what we cooked, even coming to love the process of cooking again, as we spent most of that time inspiring each other to come up with new ideas. No matter how you eat, nothing can be more boring than alternating the same exact dishes week after week.

Low-Carb Essentials is my seventh cookbook to date, and I am beyond excited to share these delicious and palate-inspiring recipes, but I cannot stress enough—our success was, and still is, because we never fell into that dreaded pitfall of eating uninspired meals. Let these recipes be your building blocks, eventually evolving to become *essentials* to your own success.

CREATE YOUR OWN ESSENTIALS

I am like a mad scientist in the kitchen. I love to invent and reinvent dishes. I've got to make things my own. Oftentimes, these experiments involve produce and herbs grown in our garden, however all of the ingredients in this book should be readily available at any grocery store.

We try to suggest new ideas in my "Helpful Tips" section within each recipe as often as possible, but sometimes we simply cannot fit every bit of information that comes to mind.

Should you be inclined to substitute any of the ingredients listed elsewhere in this book with produce or products of your own choosing, be sure to read the labels. Check the carb counts! Look for added sugar in the ingredients list. You don't want to stop the fat-burning machine once you've got it going!

We try to keep things as fresh as possible with our recipes, but there are a few ingredients you may have questions about, so I will go into more detail on them in this section.

UNSALTED BUTTER

The recipes in this book were tested with unsalted butter, however you can feel free to use salted butter in any savory dish. The impact on flavor will be too minimal to make a difference. That said, we don't recommend using salted butter in our baked goods, as they are truly better without the added salt.

SUGAR SUBSTITUTES

Nothing else has been so hotly discussed in the news or Internet over my years on a low-carb lifestyle as sugar substitutes. Opinions vary about certain products falling into this category, and rightly so. It is only natural for us to question and, yes, even demand more information on what we put into our bodies. Sugar substitutes often cause people to wonder what is or isn't naturally derived, and for those conscious of eating only natural foods (as we try to do on low carb), this is wholly understandable.

As a chef, I tend to vote with my palate. It was over a decade ago that I chose to use Splenda as my personal sugar substitute of choice, and have stuck with it ever since. This is simply my own preference. Your choice of sugar substitute is left entirely up to you.

There is a remarkable amount of sugar substitutes available in stores today, many of them entirely natural. This luxury simply did not exist back when my family lost the majority of our weight. Splenda, back then, had just hit the shelves, and any other alternatives came in either blue or pink packets. These days, you have a plethora to choose from, including erythritol, stevia, monk fruit, and agave nectar, among the many products. Others are marketed under many different brand names, such as EZ-Sweetz, Nevella, Truvia, Stevia Blend, Swerve, Organic Zero, and Just Like Sugar. The one type of sugar substitute I recommend against is xylitol, as from what I understand it can cause digestive discomfort and is also poisonous to dogs.

It's important to remember that sugar substitutes are among some of the most scrutinized and studied foods on the planet (for instance, no one is studying celery under a microscope). When in doubt, read these studies and the conclusions of those who publish them, then draw your own conclusion. I made mine long ago and feel comfortable knowing that I've eliminated both sugar and corn syrup from my life. While controversy continues to surround sugar substitutes, it is generally well accepted that eating excess sugar can raise your risk for diabetes and other diseases, especially for those who are overweight.

Regardless of your preference in sweeteners, please check to make sure it is "heat stable" before attempting to bake with it. Aspartame, for instance (which I do NOT recommend), is not heat stable and will lose its sweetness at a high enough temperature.

The recipes in this book that call for sugar substitute are all measured equal to sugar in order to make them easy to follow, no matter which substitute you prefer. If you are using a brand of sugar substitute that does not measure the same as sugar, simply follow the directions on the package to measure out the correct amount for that particular brand.

Liquid versions of the sweeteners listed above tend to contain the least amount of carbohydrates, as they require no fillers to add bulk. These also usually measure the least like sugar, so be sure to follow their directions for measuring!

Finally, I would like to make one last recommendation. If you have purchased this book with the goal to eat less or no gluten, and not to watch your weight, you can make the choice to use real sugar in my recipes. This is also perfectly acceptable. In the past, I have noticed that many of my followers buy my books purely because of gluten allergies or sensitivities. In this case, if you happen to have no issue with weight, are not at risk for diabetes, and feel comfortable with eating sugar, by all means do so.

I can't say it enough…your choice of sweetener is YOUR CHOICE.

ALMOND FLOUR

This is the only kind of "flour" we used in the making of this book, which can be purchased in most grocery stores, usually found in the baking, organic, or gluten-free sections. Since store-bought almond flour or "almond meal" can be more expensive than preparing it at home, and tends to dry out once baked, we prefer to make our own.

It is also incredibly easy to prepare: Simply grind sliced or whole raw almonds in a food processor on high for about 3 minutes. Once they've attained a grainy, flour-like consistency, keep stored in an airtight container for up to 1 week on the counter, or for several months in the freezer. Blanched almonds can also be used; these are white and have no hull, making for cleaner "white" flour-like looks, but no difference in flavor. For even smoother consistency, grind small batches of pre-ground almonds through a coffee grinder.

While almonds do contain fat (something that white flour does not), this fat happens to be the good (monounsaturated) kind and doesn't deserve to be sneered at. Our baked goods at first glance might seem high in fat due to our preference for almond flour, however these numbers hold little importance when you take into consideration where the fat comes from. Studies have even shown that a serving a day can help boost weight loss.

NUTRITIONAL INFORMATION

The nutritional analysis provided in these recipes is meant only as a reference. It was compiled to the best of our ability using nutritional analysis software with an extremely large database of ingredients. Due to variance in the sizes of vegetables, brands of certain foods, or fat content of meat, your calculations may vary.

Calculations are for each serving of the finished dish. Calories in this book were rounded to the nearest 5, and all other amounts were rounded to the nearest .5 of a gram. Optional garnishes or variations were not included in the calculations. Recipes that include the use of another recipe (such as frosting for a cake) already include the nutritional information for the additional recipe as part of the overall dish.

Though we provide the nutritional information, our family has always made it a point to not count each and every gram of carbohydrates or calories. It is our belief that if you stock your home full of great natural foods and do your best to not "cheat," you'll be eating well enough to see results. I've found that, for many people, counting carbs can lead you to eat worse when trying to save up or "bank" those extra carbs in order to eat something you probably shouldn't be eating at all. Starving yourself all day to eat an entire pie before bedtime has never been, and never will be, a good choice.

We suggest you set yourself free from those numbers altogether and eat only what is *essential* for success. Yeah, we know, we know, it is a tough urge to let go of, but trust us—it'll do wonders for your sanity! Get too caught up with counting, and eventually you'll find yourself doing long division on the walls.

NET CARBS

You will notice a number labeled "Net Carbs" in our nutritional information. Net carbs are the carbohydrates that are actually absorbed by your body—the ones that actually affect your blood sugar levels. If you are counting carbs…net carbs are the ones to count.

Our net carbs are determined only by subtracting fiber from the total carbohydrates in the recipe, as fiber does not get absorbed. Food products and other books subtract other things, such as "sugar alcohols," but we ONLY subtract fiber. If you ever stall along your weight-loss path, the only true way to know what is a "net carb" to you, is to remove any new foods you have added to see if that was the cause of your stall.

ESSENTIAL PANTRY INGREDIENTS

The following is a list of the most commonly used ingredients in this book and in our household. We try to keep most of these ingredients on hand at all times.

SPICE CABINET

- Baking powder
- Balsamic vinegar
- Basil
- Bay leaves
- Black pepper
- Cayenne pepper
- Chili powder
- Cinnamon
- Coconut extract
- Cumin
- Garlic powder
- Italian seasoning
- Nonstick cooking spray
- Olive oil
- Onion powder
- Oregano
- Paprika
- Red wine vinegar
- Smoked paprika
- Thyme
- Vanilla extract
- Vegetable oil

PANTRY

- Almond flour
- Canned pumpkin
- Dijon mustard
- Garlic bulbs
- Ground flax seed
- Pecans
- Red onions
- Roasted red peppers
- Spaghetti squash
- Sugar substitute
- Unsweetened baking chocolate
- Unsweetened cocoa powder
- Worcestershire sauce

FRIDGE

- Bacon
- Bell peppers
- Butter
- Cilantro
- Cream cheese
- Eggs
- Fresh herbs
- Half-and-half
- Heavy cream
- Lemons
- Limes
- Parmesan cheese
- Parsley
- Ricotta cheese

BREAKFAST

CONTENTS

INSIDE-OUT EGG SANDWICHES

SAUSAGE AND CHEESE BETWEEN EGG PATTY "BISCUITS"

They're called egg sandwiches for a reason. Because egg is the most important part! Here, I've found a fun, low-carb way to reinvent a classic breakfast sandwich that gets rid of all that heavy, bready, filler, and doubles down on the good stuff...the egg!

SHOPPING LIST

Nonstick cooking spray

1 tablespoon unsalted butter

4 large eggs

⅛ teaspoon salt

⅛ teaspoon black pepper

2 breakfast sausage patties, cooked

1 slice deluxe American cheese, halved

HELPFUL TIPS

Fresh breakfast sausage patties are best, as they do not have unnecessary filler ingredients that many pre-cooked patties can have.

Egg Patty Baking Method: Preheat oven to 350°F. Grease 4 muffin cups with butter or nonstick cooking spray, and then pour an equal amount of the egg mixture into each. Bake for 12–15 minutes, just until eggs have set.

1 For the best looking results, use 3-inch metal ring molds or cookie cutters to prepare the egg patties. Spray ring molds with nonstick cooking spray to prevent sticking. See left for an alternative method using a standard muffin pan.

2 Place 1 tablespoon of butter in a large nonstick skillet over medium heat.

3 In a mixing bowl, whisk together eggs, salt, and pepper.

4 Place 4 metal ring molds over the melted butter in the skillet. Spoon ¼ of the seasoned eggs into each.

5 Add a splash of water to the pan and immediately cover to steam the eggs inside the molds. Cook until eggs have set, about 4 minutes.

6 Remove egg patties from molds. Assemble sandwiches by placing 1 sausage patty atop an egg patty, then topping the sausage with ½ slice of American cheese.

7 Place another egg patty over the cheese to finish each sandwich. The heat of the sausage and eggs should melt the cheese, however you can also microwave the finished sandwich for 15 seconds if the ingredients have cooled.

Calories: 360 • Fat: 29.5g • Protein: 20g • Total Carbs: 0.5g – Fiber: 0g = **Net Carbs: 0.5g**

ZUCCHINI HASHBROWN PATTIES

ONE POTATO, TWO POTATO, NO-POTATO HASHBROWNS

Zucchini is a healthy, delicious, versatile vegetable. In this recipe, it really shows off its amazing acting range by stepping into a classic breakfast side dish role typically played by starchy, carb-filled potatoes. Crispy, golden brown, and packed with flavor, the award for Best-Vegetable-Actor in a Supporting Breakfast Role goes to....

SHOPPING LIST

3 large zucchini (about 1½ pounds)

½ teaspoon salt

2 large eggs, beaten

½ cup shredded sharp Cheddar cheese

½ teaspoon onion powder

¼ teaspoon black pepper

2 tablespoons vegetable oil

HELPFUL TIPS

The shredding attachment of a food processor or stand mixer can make quick work of shredding the zucchini in this recipe.

1 USING a large cheese grater, shred the zucchini into a large bowl.

2 PRESS down on the shredded zucchini and drain to remove excess moisture.

3 TOSS the zucchini with the salt and let stand 10 minutes. Press and drain the zucchini again.

4 FOLD the eggs, cheese, onion powder, and pepper into the shredded zucchini to create a hashbrown batter.

5 HEAT 1 tablespoon of the vegetable oil in a large nonstick skillet over medium-high heat.

6 USE a large spoon or ice cream scoop to transfer 4 (3-tablespoon) scoops of the batter into the hot skillet. Press down to flatten into patties.

7 COOK until golden brown, about 3 minutes on each side.

8 REPEAT with the remaining 1 tablespoon of vegetable oil and remaining batter, making 8 hashbrown patties.

Calories: 180 • Fat: 14g • Protein: 8.5g • Total Carbs: 6g – Fiber: 2g = **Net Carbs: 4g**

CREAMY SCRAMBLED EGGS WITH CHIVES

BREAKFAST

FRENCH-STYLE EGGS THAT CAN'T BE BEAT

Viva la eggs! This delicate variation on a scrambled standard is so soft and creamy, you'll wonder why I never told you about it before. I was being sneaky. I'm sorry. But I can't keep this simple secret to myself any longer. Fresh chives add the subtle flavor of onion that will have you saying, "oui, oui!"

SHOPPING LIST

4 large eggs

2 tablespoons half-and-half

¼ teaspoon salt

⅛ teaspoon black pepper

1 pinch garlic powder

2 tablespoons unsalted butter, divided

2 tablespoons chopped fresh chives

HELPFUL TIPS

A flexible rubber spatula works best for scrambling eggs, allowing you to easily reach every corner of the skillet.

1 WHISK the eggs, half-and-half, salt, pepper, and garlic powder until smooth and frothy.

2 MELT 1 tablespoon of the butter in a nonstick skillet over medium heat.

3 POUR the eggs into the skillet and use a spatula to constantly scrape the bottom of the pan.

4 ONCE the eggs begin to cook, reduce heat to low.

5 CONTINUE scraping the bottom of the pan as you stir the cooked egg into the raw egg. Always keep the eggs in motion.

6 ONCE the eggs are mostly scrambled, but still creamy, remove from heat.

7 STIR in the chopped chives and remaining 1 tablespoon of butter. Serve immediately.

Calories: 265 • Fat: 23g • Protein: 13.5g • Total Carbs: 1.5g – Fiber: 0g = **Net Carbs: 1.5g**

DENVER OMELET BITES

WHOLE EGG "MUFFINS" WITH HAM, ONIONS, AND PEPPERS

Tweaking a recipe isn't always about replacing one ingredient with another; sometimes it's simply about finding a fun, convenient way to eat it faster. By throwing everything you love about Denver omelets into a muffin pan, you get all the flavor of an American diner favorite in adorable little handheld breakfast bites. No plate, no fork, no knife…no problem!

SHOPPING LIST

Nonstick cooking spray

½ cup diced cooked ham

⅓ cup finely diced yellow onion

6 large eggs

¼ cup finely diced green bell pepper

½ cup shredded sharp Cheddar cheese

HELPFUL TIPS

We like to use silicone muffin pans to make these, as you can invert the silicone and pop the cooked eggs right out without any mess.

1 PLACE oven rack in the center position and preheat oven to 375°F. Spray a 6-cup muffin pan with nonstick cooking spray.

2 DIVIDE an equal amount of the ham and onion into each muffin cup.

3 CRACK an egg over the ham and onion in each cup, taking care not to break any yolks.

4 BAKE for 12–14 minutes, or until egg whites are firm.

5 TOP each cooked egg with equal amounts of the bell pepper and cheese.

6 RETURN to the oven for about 1–2 minutes, just until the cheese is melted.

7 LET cool for 2 minutes before using a rubber spatula or fork to release from the tin. Serve hot.

Calories: 130 • Fat: 9g • Protein: 10.5g • Total Carbs: 2g – Fiber: 0g = **Net Carbs: 2g**

BLUEBERRY DANISH MUFFINS

WITH CREAM CHEESE FILLING AND STREUSEL TOPPING

These muffins are so good, it would be easy to understand the skeptical, raised eyebrow you might get when you say they're actually good FOR you. But blueberries are some of the most nutrient-dense berries on the planet. By folding them into a healthy, high-protein, almond flour batter, you've got a great start to an even better day.

SHOPPING LIST

4 large eggs

¼ cup water

1 tablespoon vanilla extract

2 cups blanched almond flour

½ cup sugar substitute

1 tablespoon baking powder

½ cup fresh blueberries

CHEESE FILLING

8 ounces cream cheese, softened

1 large egg, beaten

½ cup fresh blueberries

STREUSEL TOPPING

¼ cup blanched almond flour

2 tablespoons sugar substitute

1½ tablespoons unsalted butter, cold

¼ teaspoon ground cinnamon

HELPFUL TIPS

We like to use silicone muffin pans to make these, as you can invert the silicone, and pop the muffin right out.

1 PLACE oven rack in the center position and preheat oven to 375°F. Line a 12-cup muffin pan with paper liners.

2 IN a large bowl, beat 4 eggs until frothy. Add the water and vanilla extract, and whisk to combine.

3 IN a separate bowl, mix the 2 cups almond flour, sugar substitute, and baking powder. Whisk the dry ingredients into the wet ingredients until all is combined.

4 FOLD ½ cup of blueberries into the batter.

5 FILL the prepared muffin cups with equal amounts of the finished batter, filling each about ⅔ of the way full.

6 CREATE the Cheese Filling by whisking together cream cheese and egg. Spoon equal amounts of the mixture onto the batter in the prepared muffin cups. Top evenly with the second ½ cup of blueberries.

7 COMBINE all Streusel Topping ingredients, using a fork to cut the butter into the topping. Crumble equally over the top of each muffin.

8 BAKE for 20–25 minutes, or until muffins are firm and spongy, and a toothpick inserted into the center of one comes out mostly clean. Let cool for 10 minutes before removing from the pan. Serve warm or chilled. Store refrigerated.

Calories: 245 • Fat: 20g • Protein: 9g • Total Carbs: 9g – Fiber: 3g = **Net Carbs: 6g**

CAPRESE EGG WHITE FRITTATA

WITH TOMATOES, FRESH MOZZARELLA, AND BASIL

Guess who's coming to breakfast? A simple, savory, Italian staple, Caprese salad is a classic that's just too fresh and delicious to wait until lunch or dinner to enjoy. So here, I've combined those traditional flavors with a light, fluffy frittata. A perfect way to start the day. Now, if I could only find a way to have a Caprese salad for dessert….

SHOPPING LIST

1 tablespoon olive oil

8 large egg whites

¼ teaspoon salt

¼ teaspoon black pepper

⅛ teaspoon garlic powder

⅛ teaspoon baking powder

4 thick slices tomato, patted dry

4 slices fresh mozzarella cheese

8 leaves basil

1 tablespoon extra virgin olive oil

2 teaspoons balsamic vinegar

HELPFUL TIPS

Always be sure to purchase actual balsamic vinegar and not balsamic "glaze," as glazes are full of added sugar.

1 PLACE oven rack in the second highest position. Set broiler to low.

2 HEAT the olive oil in a large ovenproof skillet over medium heat.

3 IN a mixing bowl, whisk together the egg whites, salt, pepper, garlic powder, and baking powder.

4 POUR the egg mixture into the skillet. Using a rubber spatula, gently push the cooked eggs from one side of the pan to the other to allow more of the raw eggs to reach the bottom of the pan. Continue doing this until the top of the eggs are only slightly runny.

5 ARRANGE the sliced tomatoes and sliced mozzarella cheese evenly over the surface of the frittata, overlapping each other, if there is not enough room.

6 BROIL for 3–4 minutes, just until cheese has melted and eggs have set.

7 ARRANGE the basil leaves over the frittata and drizzle with extra virgin olive oil and balsamic vinegar before serving.

Calories: 180 • Fat: 12g • Protein: 15.5g • Total Carbs: 2.5g – Fiber: 0g = **Net Carbs: 2.5g**

FARMHOUSE FRITTATA

WITH MUSHROOMS, SPINACH, AND FETA CHEESE

The natural, earthy flavor of mushrooms, fresh spinach, and rich, tangy, feta cheese combine in a light, airy frittata to whisk your taste buds off on a tour of the countryside. It's all the pleasures of a farm-fresh meal, in the comforts of your own home. After breakfast, kick back, close your eyes, and pretend your ottoman is a bale of hay.

SHOPPING LIST

1 tablespoon olive oil

1 tablespoon unsalted butter

4 ounces sliced button mushrooms

2 cups fresh spinach leaves

½ teaspoon minced garlic

6 large eggs

¼ teaspoon salt

¼ teaspoon black pepper

⅛ teaspoon baking powder

½ cup crumbled feta cheese

¼ cup diced tomato, for garnish

HELPFUL TIPS

Frozen chopped spinach (⅔ cup) can be used in place of the fresh spinach in this recipe.

1 PREHEAT oven to 325°F.

2 HEAT the olive oil and butter in a large ovenproof skillet over medium-high heat.

3 ADD the mushrooms to the skillet and sauté until they are almost tender, about 5 minutes.

4 REDUCE heat to medium low. Add the spinach and garlic to skillet and sauté until spinach has cooked down, about 2 minutes.

5 IN a mixing bowl, whisk together the eggs, salt, pepper, and baking powder. Pour over the vegetables in the skillet.

6 USING a rubber spatula, gently push the cooked eggs from one side of the pan to the other to allow more of the raw eggs to reach the bottom of the pan. Continue doing this until the top of the eggs are only slightly runny.

7 SPRINKLE the feta cheese over top of the frittata and bake for 10 minutes, or until eggs begin to puff up. Serve garnished with diced tomato.

Calories: 220 • Fat: 17.5g • Protein: 14g • Total Carbs: 3.5g − Fiber: 1.5g = **Net Carbs: 2g**

SAUSAGE AND SWEET POTATO HASH

TOP WITH A FRIED EGG FOR AN AMAZING BREAKFAST

This sweet and savory breakfast hash is filling and full of protein—a great meal to get you through a long day's work, or a great way to start a relaxing day at home. A cup of coffee and a crossword puzzle make great side dishes. What's a four-letter word for "Come up with a plan?" Hash.

SHOPPING LIST

1 tablespoon olive oil

1 pound bulk breakfast sausage

1 sweet potato, diced

½ cup diced red onion

½ cup diced red bell pepper

1 tablespoon chopped fresh sage

½ teaspoon minced garlic

¼ teaspoon dried thyme

¼ teaspoon chili powder

¼ teaspoon salt

¼ teaspoon black pepper

1 HEAT oil in a large skillet over medium-high heat.

2 PLACE the sausage in the skillet and crumble as it browns. Cook until mostly browned, about 5 minutes.

3 ADD all remaining ingredients to the skillet and sauté 5–8 minutes, until sweet potatoes are fork-tender. Serve as is, or topped with a fried egg for a full breakfast.

HELPFUL TIPS

If the skillet gets too dry before the potatoes are tender, simply add a few tablespoons of tap water to the hash to prevent it from burning.

Calories: 300 • Fat: 24g • Protein: 15.5g • Total Carbs: 5.5g – Fiber: 1g = **Net Carbs: 4.5g**

PUMPKIN PECAN PANCAKES

A SHORT STACK OF FALL FLAVORS

Nothing says fall like the changing colors of the leaves…. But pumpkin is a close second, and it tastes way better on the breakfast table in a stack of piping hot, pecan pancakes. So, have the best of both worlds: look out the window at the beautiful leaves while you tuck into these delicious almond flour and flax seed flapjacks. And if the leaves don't change color where you live, trust me, you'll forget all about it after the first bite.

SHOPPING LIST

Nonstick cooking spray

2 large eggs

½ cup blanched almond flour

¼ cup pure canned pumpkin

¼ cup ground flax seed

¼ cup sugar substitute

¼ cup water

1 tablespoon vanilla extract

1 teaspoon baking powder

1 teaspoon pumpkin pie spice

¼ cup pecans, coarsely chopped

HELPFUL TIPS

Make a Maple Butter to top by whipping together 4 tablespoons of softened butter, 2 tablespoons sugar substitute, and ¼ teaspoon maple extract.

1 SPRAY a griddle or large nonstick skillet with nonstick cooking spray and heat over medium heat.

2 USING a rubber spatula, stir together all ingredients, except pecans, until a well-blended batter is formed. Transfer to a large measuring cup.

3 POUR 8 medium-sized cakes onto the hot griddle.

4 COOK on one side for 2 minutes.

5 SPRINKLE each cake with an equal amount of the chopped pecans and let cook for 1 more minute, just until golden brown on the bottom.

6 FLIP and cook for 2 additional minutes. Serve topped with a pat of butter or sugar-free whipped cream.

Calories: 250 • Fat: 20g • Protein: 10g • Total Carbs: 12g − Fiber: 7g = **Net Carbs: 5g**

LOADED LOW-CARB GRITS

SOUTHERN-STYLE GRITS, MADE ENTIRELY GRAIN-FREE

No dish screams "The South!" louder and prouder than grits. With this almond flour alternative to a southern classic, you can join in the chorus without all the carbs. Rich, creamy, and loaded with Cheddar cheese and bacon, not even 'My Cousin Vinny' could resist.

SHOPPING LIST

2 cups blanched almond flour

2 cups water

2 tablespoons unsalted butter

¼ teaspoon salt

1 cup shredded sharp Cheddar cheese

6 slices bacon, cooked and crumbled

2 green onions, sliced

1 ADD the almond flour, water, butter, and salt to a saucepan over medium-high heat and whisk to combine. Stirring constantly, bring up to a simmer.

2 CONTINUE stirring as the mixture cooks for 5–6 minutes, or until it begins to thicken.

3 REMOVE grits from heat and stir in Cheddar cheese and bacon. Let cool for 5 minutes as the mixture continues to thicken.

4 SERVE topped with sliced green onions.

HELPFUL TIPS

Load these mock grits up any way you please! Crumbled breakfast sausage and freshly chopped sage are great in place of the bacon and green onions.

Calories: 290 • Fat: 26g • Protein: 12g • Total Carbs: 6.5g − Fiber: 3g = **Net Carbs: 3.5g**

CHOCOLATE WAFFLES

WITH CHOCOLATE IN THE BATTER AND A CHOCOLATE DUSTING

Chocolate Waffles?! Is it your birthday? Maybe. Is it Christmas? Could be. Is it breakfast? Dessert? Is it breakfast FOR dessert? Or dessert for breakfast? I'm not sure when you're reading this, or how you specifically define breakfast or dessert. It could be ALL of those things at once…and let's face it, when you're eating chocolate waffles, it just might be!

SHOPPING LIST

Nonstick cooking spray

½ cup almond flour

⅓ cup heavy cream

⅓ cup sugar substitute

2 large eggs, beaten

3 tablespoons ground flax seed

4 teaspoons unsweetened cocoa powder

1 tablespoon vegetable oil

1 teaspoon vanilla extract

½ teaspoon baking powder

CHOCOLATE DUSTING

2 tablespoons sugar substitute

1 teaspoon unsweetened cocoa powder

HELPFUL TIPS

Making waffles can get messy! It is entirely normal for some batter to spill out until you get used to the proper amount for your maker. Placing the waffle iron on a sheet pan makes for much easier cleanup.

1 SPRAY an electric waffle iron with nonstick cooking spray and let preheat.

2 IN a large bowl, whisk together all ingredients, except the Chocolate Dusting. Mix until a thick but smooth consistency is reached. If the batter is not smooth or resembles a thick dough, simply add a small amount of tap water.

3 POUR ¼ cup of batter over the center of the waffle iron (more or less batter, depending on the size of the iron) and close the lid.

4 COOK for about 5 minutes, or until steam is no longer escaping the sides of the iron. Remove finished waffle and repeat until all batter is used.

5 COMBINE Chocolate Dusting ingredients and sprinkle over the hot waffles before serving. Top with butter, fresh berries, or whipped cream, if desired.

Calories: 290 • Fat: 25g • Protein: 10.5g • Total Carbs: 11g − Fiber: 5g = **Net Carbs: 6g**

BERRY BASIL FRUIT SALAD

A SWEET BREAKFAST SIDE DISH WITH A SAVORY TWIST

It's easy to forget when cooking, that oftentimes, nature only needs a little nudge. Here, she's done most of the work for us. Berries are bright, beautiful, and bursting with vitamins, minerals, and antioxidants. Basil is a cousin of mint, so it makes perfect sense that it perfectly compliments the sweetness of the berries. You'll feel great starting any morning off with this fresh, lively, fruit salad, and even better about how little work you had to do to make it.

SHOPPING LIST

1½ cups sliced strawberries

1 cup raspberries

1 cup blueberries

6 basil leaves, thinly sliced

Juice of ½ lemon

1 tablespoon sugar substitute

2 teaspoons olive oil

1 IN a large mixing bowl, toss all ingredients to combine.

2 FOR best flavor, cover and refrigerate for 30 minutes before serving.

HELPFUL TIPS

Though it may sound strange, a pinch of black pepper really adds another dimension to this recipe. Black pepper goes just as well with the berries as the basil.

Calories: 50 • Fat: 2g • Protein: 0.5g • Total Carbs: 8.5g − Fiber: 2.5g = **Net Carbs: 6g**

CONFETTI QUICHE

CRUSTLESS QUICHE THAT WILL HAVE YOU "COOKING WITH COLOR"

You've gotta cook with color! This is a useful rule of thumb, especially when it comes to produce, because oftentimes, the color of a fruit or vegetable is directly related to its nutrient content. The brighter and more colorful, the better it is for you. In this quiche recipe, I've done away with the crust, and opted instead for fresh, lively, colorful veggies.

SHOPPING LIST

Nonstick cooking spray

2 teaspoons olive oil

¼ cup diced red onion

¼ cup diced yellow bell pepper

¼ cup diced red bell pepper

6 large eggs

¼ cup heavy cream

¾ teaspoon salt

¼ teaspoon black pepper

¼ teaspoon garlic powder

⅛ teaspoon ground nutmeg

2 cups shredded sharp white
   Cheddar cheese (see tip)

2 tablespoons chopped fresh parsley

1 PREHEAT oven to 350°F. Spray an 8-inch square baking dish or 9-inch pie pan with nonstick cooking spray.

2 HEAT oil in a small skillet over medium heat.

3 PLACE onion, yellow bell pepper, and red bell pepper in the skillet and sauté for 3 minutes, just until vegetables begin to soften. Let cool.

4 IN a mixing bowl, whisk together the eggs, heavy cream, salt, pepper, garlic powder, and nutmeg.

5 FOLD the cheese, parsley, and sautéed vegetable mixture into the eggs. Pour all into the prepared baking dish.

6 BAKE for 40 minutes, or until the top of the quiche is golden brown and a toothpick inserted into it comes out mostly clean. Let cool for 5 minutes before slicing to serve warm. If you prefer, cover and refrigerate at least 2 hours to serve chilled.

HELPFUL TIPS

Any kind of Cheddar cheese can be used, however I suggest using white Cheddar, as it doesn't make the quiche too dark to see all of the colorful vegetables.

Calories: 195 • Fat: 15.5g • Protein: 12g • Total Carbs: 1.5g – Fiber: 0g = **Net Carbs: 1.5g**

BLT EGG CUPS

EGGS BAKED IN TOMATOES WITH BACON AND LETTUCE

*Tomatoes are so delicious and ubiquitous, they're in practically everything!
So I thought it was about time to flip the script and start putting things
IN tomatoes! First up: bacon and eggs. A hollowed out tomato makes
the perfect baking cup, and a fun, fresh spin on the beloved BLT.*

SHOPPING LIST

4 medium tomatoes

Nonstick cooking spray

Salt and black pepper

4 strips bacon, cooked and
    crumbled, divided

4 large eggs

4 large leaves lettuce

SAUCE

2 tablespoons mayonnaise

½ teaspoon Dijon mustard

⅛ teaspoon paprika

⅛ teaspoon black pepper

HELPFUL TIPS

Reserve the tops of the tomatoes, and
place in the oven in the last 5 minutes
of cooking to create a nice (inedible)
garnish to lean alongside each cup.

1 PREHEAT oven to 400°F. Line a sheet pan with
   parchment paper.

2 SLICE a thin sliver from the bottom of each
   tomato to ensure that they will stand upright
   and level.

3 SLICE tops from tomatoes. Use a spoon to scoop
   the flesh and seeds out of the center of each
   tomato, leaving at least ¼ inch of flesh around
   the walls.

4 PLACE the hollow tomatoes on the prepared sheet
   pan and spray with nonstick cooking spray inside
   and out. Lightly season with salt and pepper.

5 SPRINKLE ½ of the crumbled bacon evenly into
   the 4 tomatoes. Reserve the remaining bacon
   for garnish.

6 CRACK 1 whole egg into each tomato.

7 BAKE for 15 minutes, or until the whites of the
   eggs are firm.

8 IN a small mixing bowl, whisk together all Sauce
   ingredients, until combined.

9 SERVE each baked egg cup atop a large leaf of
   lettuce, topped with 2 teaspoons of the sauce and
   an equal amount of the remaining bacon.

Calories: 205 • Fat: 16g • Protein: 10.5g • Total Carbs: 5.5g – Fiber: 1.5g = **Net Carbs: 4g**

LUNCH

CONTENTS

MAC-FREE MINESTRONE SOUP

SO GOOD THAT YOU WON'T MISS THE MAC

This filler-free traditional soup recipe is packed with protein and full of flavor. You won't even notice it's noodle-less! In fact, "minestrone" means "vegetable soup," so think of the lack of pasta as a respectful return to form for a well-loved classic.

LUNCH

SHOPPING LIST

1 tablespoon olive oil

3 stalks celery, diced

½ cup diced red onion

2 teaspoons minced garlic

4 cups beef broth or stock

1 (14.5-ounce) can diced
   tomatoes, with liquid

1 (15-ounce) can black soy
   beans, drained (see tip)

1 (8-ounce) can tomato sauce

2 cups chopped green beans
   (fresh or frozen)

2 zucchini, chopped

2 tablespoons chopped fresh basil

¾ teaspoon dried oregano

¼ teaspoon salt

¼ teaspoon black pepper

Shredded Parmesan cheese, for garnish

1 HEAT the oil in a stockpot over medium-high heat.

2 ADD the celery, onion, and garlic to the pot and sauté for 3 minutes, or until onions are translucent and garlic is fragrant.

3 STIR in all remaining ingredients, except Parmesan cheese.

4 BRING up to a simmer. Cover and reduce heat to low.

5 LET simmer for 15–20 minutes, just until vegetables are tender.

6 SEASON with any additional salt and pepper to taste before serving. Serve topped with shredded Parmesan cheese.

HELPFUL TIPS

Canned black soy beans are sold in many grocery stores in the organic or health foods section, though they may also be found alongside the other canned beans.

Calories: 115 • Fat: 4.5g • Protein: 7g • Total Carbs: 13g – Fiber: 6g = **Net Carbs: 7g**

SUPERFOOD SLAW

WITH KALE, PUMPKIN SEEDS, AND GORGONZOLA

This cool and crisp slaw is delicious as a side dish or a light, nutritious, lunch. In fact, the original Dutch word for kale is "boerenkool." It's got "cool" right in its name! Kale and pepitas are considered among the world's healthiest foods; both rich in essential vitamins and minerals. There's so much Super in this Superfood Slaw, it'll make you think you can fly. But please don't try. You definitely cannot fly.

SHOPPING LIST

DRESSING

3 tablespoons cider vinegar

2 tablespoons extra virgin olive oil

2 tablespoons chopped fresh parsley

1 tablespoon sugar substitute

¼ teaspoon salt

¼ teaspoon black pepper

SALAD

1 (12-ounce) bag broccoli slaw

1 bunch kale, stems removed
   and chopped

⅓ cup crumbled Gorgonzola cheese

¼ cup roasted pepitas (shelled
   pumpkin seeds)

1   ADD all Dressing ingredients to a large mixing bowl and whisk to combine.

2   ADD the Salad ingredients into the Dressing, tossing until well coated.

3   COVER and refrigerate for at least 2 hours before serving.

HELPFUL TIPS

Most broccoli slaw mixes include a small amount of shaved carrots. Carrots are high in natural carbs and are therefore not recommended for the first few weeks of low-carb. Substituting angel hair coleslaw cabbage (which is sold in stores without the carrots of other slaw mixes) in place of the broccoli slaw will lower the net carbs by 1g.

Calories: 120 • Fat: 8.5g • Protein: 6g • Total Carbs: 7.5g – Fiber: 2.5g = **Net Carbs: 5g**

LUNCH

AVOCADO CAESAR SALAD

WITH CRUMBLED BACON AND PARMESAN "CROUTON" CRISPS

In this variation on a lovable, lunchtime indulgence, the addition of an "alligator pear" makes for a creamy, heart-healthy spin on classic Caesar dressing, and the crunchy, baked, Parmesan crisps are so delicious you'll wonder why all croutons aren't made of cheese. Also, yes: "alligator pear" is a nickname for avocado.

SHOPPING LIST

DRESSING

1 Hass avocado, pitted and peeled

¼ cup shredded Parmesan cheese

2 tablespoons extra virgin olive oil

1 tablespoon lemon juice

2 teaspoons anchovy paste

1 teaspoon minced garlic

1 teaspoon Dijon mustard

¼ teaspoon black pepper

PARMESAN CRISPS

½ cup shredded Parmesan cheese

½ teaspoon Italian seasoning

¼ teaspoon garlic powder

SALAD

1 large head romaine lettuce, chopped

4 slices bacon, cooked and crumbled

HELPFUL TIPS

You can also serve this salad topped with ordinary shredded or shaved Parmesan cheese to skip the added prep of the Parmesan Crisps.

1 ADD all Dressing ingredients to a food processor.

2 PULSE Dressing until smooth and creamy. Dressing will be thick. Add cold water, a teaspoon at a time, until the dressing has thinned to your desired consistency. Cover and refrigerate for at least 30 minutes before serving.

3 As the Dressing chills, begin preparing the Parmesan Crisps. Preheat oven to 400°F. Line a sheet pan with parchment paper.

4 PLACE 16 (½-tablespoon) mounds of the shredded Parmesan cheese on the prepared sheet pan, leaving 2 inches of space between each. Sprinkle evenly with Italian seasoning and garlic powder.

5 BAKE crisps for 6 minutes, or until golden brown. Let cool at least 10 minutes to crisp up.

6 ASSEMBLE the salad by placing the chopped lettuce in a large salad bowl.

7 POUR the chilled Dressing over the lettuce and toss to evenly coat.

8 SERVE topped with the crumbled bacon and Parmesan Crisps.

Calories: 200 • Fat: 19.5g • Protein: 8g • Total Carbs: 5g – Fiber: 3g = **Net Carbs: 2g**

WISCONSIN CHEESE SOUP

ENJOY WHILE WEARING YOUR NOVELTY CHEESE HAT (NOT REQUIRED)

You don't have to make the trek to the Midwest to warm up with a smooth, savory bowl of cheese soup. You can go from prep to serve before halftime in the Packers game is over! You don't even have to wait until winter. This soup is delicious no matter what color the leaves on the trees are outside. In fact, you don't even have to use a spoon. Go ahead; pick the bowl up, and take a sip…I won't tell.

LUNCH

SHOPPING LIST

¼ cup unsalted butter

2 stalks celery, diced

½ cup diced yellow onion

½ cup diced red bell pepper

3 cups chicken broth or stock

¼ teaspoon ground mustard

¼ teaspoon paprika

¼ teaspoon salt

¼ teaspoon black pepper

1 cup heavy cream

2 cups shredded sharp Cheddar cheese

1 HEAT the butter in a sauce pot over medium-high heat.

2 ADD the celery, onion, and bell pepper to the pot and sauté for 3 minutes, or until onions are translucent.

3 POUR in chicken broth and add the ground mustard, paprika, salt, and pepper.

4 BRING up to a boil. Stir in heavy cream and, stirring constantly, bring back up to a simmer.

5 REMOVE from the heat and whisk in Cheddar cheese, whisking until the soup is smooth and creamy. Season with any additional salt and pepper to taste before serving.

HELPFUL TIPS

For a more adult flavor, substitute 12 ounces of a low-carb beer (such as Michelob Ultra) in place of 1½ cups of the chicken stock. This will add less than ½ net carb per serving.

Calories: 235 • Fat: 21g • Protein: 9.5g • Total Carbs: 2.5g – Fiber: 0g = **Net Carbs: 2.5g**

FRESH MEX CHILI

CHUNKY CHILI WITH CRISP VEGETABLES AND DICED AVOCADO

This funky, chunky, twist on chili leaves the beans on the sidelines and lets fresh veggies get into the game for a change. Fresh, creamy avocado and a dollop of cool sour cream top it all off to cut the heat. Just another example of how "cooking with color" is good for the body and the soul.

LUNCH

SHOPPING LIST

1 tablespoon vegetable oil

1 pound ground beef

½ cup diced red onion

¾ cup diced red bell pepper

2 jalapeño peppers, seeded and diced

1 tablespoon chili powder

2 teaspoons minced garlic

½ teaspoon ground cumin

1 (28-ounce) can diced tomatoes, with liquid

1 small zucchini, diced

1 yellow squash, diced

¼ cup chopped cilantro

Juice of ½ lime

¾ teaspoon salt

½ teaspoon black pepper

1 avocado, chopped

¼ cup sour cream

1 HEAT the oil in a stockpot over medium-high heat.

2 BROWN the ground beef in the pot, crumbling it as it cooks, about 7 minutes. Drain excess grease.

3 REDUCE heat to medium. Add the onion, bell pepper, jalapeño, chili powder, garlic, and cumin to the ground beef. Sauté for 5 minutes, just until the peppers begin to soften.

4 ADD the diced tomatoes with liquid, zucchini, yellow squash, cilantro, lime juice, salt, and pepper to the pot. Bring up to a simmer, cover, reduce heat to low, and let simmer for 5 minutes, just until squash is crisp-tender.

5 SERVE topped with diced avocado and a dollop of sour cream.

HELPFUL TIPS

To keep the diced avocado looking fresh and green, toss in a small amount of lime juice after cutting.

Calories: 310 • Fat: 20g • Protein: 24.5g • Total Carbs: 9g – Fiber: 3g = **Net Carbs: 6g**

LUNCH

ROTISSERIE CHICKEN SOUP

HEARTY CHICKEN SOUP, ALMOST MADE FROM SCRATCH

The rotisserie method of roasting meats dates all the way back to medieval times. But just because we don't all have "spit-jacks" in our castle kitchens, doesn't mean our grocery stores do not! This recipe may start with a cooked bird, but it makes something entirely new from it. One spoonful of this robust, flavorful soup and you'll agree: it's fit for a king!

SHOPPING LIST

1 store-bought cooked rotisserie chicken

2 bay leaves

1 tablespoon olive oil

8 ounces sliced button mushrooms

4 stalks celery, sliced

1 small yellow onion, diced

2 teaspoons minced garlic

½ cup heavy cream

2 tablespoons chopped fresh parsley

¾ teaspoon dried thyme

½ teaspoon salt

¼ teaspoon black pepper

HELPFUL TIPS

You can skip making the stock from scratch while still using the delicious rotisserie chicken meat to make this soup. Simply substitute 8–12 cups of store-bought stock or broth and skip steps 2–4 in this recipe.

1 REMOVE skin from rotisserie chicken and set aside. Pull all meat from the chicken and shred into bite-sized pieces. Cover and refrigerate shredded chicken meat as you prepare the stock.

2 PLACE chicken carcass, reserved skin, and bay leaves into a large stockpot over high heat. Cover with about 3 quarts of water, or until the entire carcass is submerged.

3 BRING water to a boil. Reduce heat to a low simmer, cover, and simmer for 90 minutes.

4 DISCARD bones and skin. Strain stock through a mesh strainer for a cleaner broth.

5 HEAT the oil in a clean pot over medium-high heat.

6 ADD the mushrooms, celery, onion, and garlic to the pot and sauté for 7 minutes, or until mushrooms are tender.

7 ADD the strained chicken stock, shredded chicken meat, and all remaining ingredients.

8 BRING up to a simmer and let cook for 10 minutes. Season with any additional salt and pepper to taste before serving.

Calories: 280 • Fat: 17g • Protein: 26g • Total Carbs: 3g − Fiber: 1g = **Net Carbs: 2g**

TUNA AND "MACARONI" SALAD

WITH CAULIFLOWER MOCK-MACARONI

A perfect, protein-packed, picnic side dish. Or a power lunch. Or both! In this dish, the boost of energy you get from tuna and eggs isn't undermined by pasta. Instead, nutrient-rich, cruciferous, chameleon cauliflower steps in disguised as "mock-aroni" to fill that filling void with a jolt of vitamin C.

LUNCH

SHOPPING LIST

SALAD

1 large head cauliflower, leaves removed

2 (5-ounce) cans albacore tuna in water, drained

4 hard-boiled eggs, chopped

2 stalks celery, finely diced

½ cup grape tomatoes, halved

¼ cup diced yellow onion

¼ cup sliced green olives

DRESSING

¾ cup mayonnaise

2 tablespoons sugar-free sweet relish

2 tablespoons chopped fresh parsley

2 teaspoons cider vinegar

¼ teaspoon salt

¼ teaspoon black pepper

1 CHOP the cauliflower into small (½-inch) pieces.

2 PLACE a large pot of water over high heat.

3 ADD the cauliflower pieces to the boiling water and cook for 5 minutes, or until tender. Drain and rinse under cold water.

4 TRANSFER the drained cauliflower to a large mixing bowl and top with all remaining Salad ingredients.

5 ADD all Dressing ingredients to a separate mixing bowl and whisk to combine.

6 GENTLY fold the finished dressing into the salad, just until everything is well coated.

7 COVER and refrigerate for at least 1 hour before serving.

HELPFUL TIPS

As with most creamy salads, the longer you let this chill, the better it will taste. That's good news for the leftovers!

Calories: 230 • Fat: 18g • Protein: 13g • Total Carbs: 5g − Fiber: 2g = **Net Carbs: 3g**

ARTICHOKE PICNIC SALAD

ANTIPASTO SALAD IN A CREAMY DRESSING

Although the word "antipasto" means "before the meal," no one would blame you for making this creamy classic a meal in its own right. Olives, onions, and tomatoes shine in a mix of traditional Italian flavors, but the true star in this salad is the artichoke. You may not be in Tuscany, but your taste buds won't know that.

SHOPPING LIST

DRESSING

½ cup mayonnaise

1 tablespoon red wine vinegar

2 tablespoons chopped fresh parsley

1 teaspoon minced garlic

1 teaspoon Dijon mustard

½ teaspoon Italian seasoning

¼ teaspoon salt

¼ teaspoon black pepper

SALAD

2 (14-ounce) cans quartered artichoke hearts, drained

½ cup whole black olives, pitted

½ cup grape tomatoes, halved

¼ cup thinly sliced red onion

1 ADD all Dressing ingredients to a large mixing bowl and whisk to combine.

2 ADD the Salad ingredients into the Dressing, folding until well coated.

3 COVER and refrigerate for at least 1 hour before serving.

HELPFUL TIPS

When draining canned artichokes, it is best to give them a good rinse as well, as it helps remove the sodium and flavor of the brine used in the canning process.

FIRENZE STEAK SALAD

SLICED STEAK AND SHAVED PARMESAN ON A BED OF ARUGULA

Sometimes less is more. Just look at the list of ingredients for this deliciously simple salad. You could probably remember them all without even writing them down. But, maybe you should write them down. Just in case. I wouldn't want you to forget any important part of this amazing taste of Tuscany!

SHOPPING LIST

1 (8-ounce) sirloin steak

Salt and black pepper

Garlic powder

2 packed cups arugula

2 ounces shaved Parmesan cheese

1 tablespoon extra virgin olive oil

2 teaspoons balsamic vinegar

1 GENEROUSLY season the steak with salt, pepper, and garlic powder.

2 GRILL, broil, or pan-fry steaks for 4 minutes on each side, or until your desired doneness. Let rest 5 minutes.

3 ARRANGE arugula on a serving platter or separate salad plates.

4 THINLY slice the cooked steak and fan out over top of the arugula.

5 TOP the entire salad with shaved Parmesan cheese. Drizzle with olive oil and balsamic vinegar before serving.

HELPFUL TIPS

While any Parmesan will work, Parmigiano Reggiano—the king of cheeses—is highly recommended for this recipe!

Calories: 380 • Fat: 23.5g • Protein: 41g • Total Carbs: 1.5g – Fiber: 0g = **Net Carbs: 1.5g**

CRISPY CHEESE TACO SHELLS

100% CHEESE TACO SHELLS FOR 100% CHEESIER TACOS

These crispy, cheesy, quick and easy, nearly no-carb taco shells are absolutely delicious! The only problem with them is, once you realize you can make a taco shell entirely out of cheese, you'll start wondering what else you can make from cheese.

LUNCH

SHOPPING LIST

1 cup shredded Cheddar cheese

1 cup shredded mozzarella cheese

HELPFUL TIPS

You can sprinkle these with chili powder as they cook to give them a little bit of a nacho cheese-style kick.

1 PLACE an 8-inch nonstick skillet over medium heat.

2 IN a mixing bowl, toss together both types of shredded cheese.

3 SPRINKLE ½ cup of the mixture across the pan in a thin layer, leaving an inch of space between the cheese and the sides of the pan.

4 COOK for 3 minutes, or until lifting an edge reveals that it is golden brown.

5 USE a fork or tongs to carefully flip the fried cheese and cook for an additional 2 minutes on the opposite side.

6 REMOVE from pan and immediately drape the fried cheese over a clean rolling pin or similar object with a cylindrical shape. Let the fried cheese cool until it hardens.

7 REPEAT this process to make 3 additional taco shells. Serve filled with your favorite taco fixings.

Calories: 195 • Fat: 14.5g • Protein: 15g • Total Carbs: 1g – Fiber: 0g = **Net Carbs: 1g**

CHILLED CAULIFLOWER AND BROCCOLI SALAD

WITH BACON, CHEDDAR CHEESE, AND SUNFLOWER SEEDS

If the kids still won't eat their vegetables, even after you tell them they're chock full of crispy bacon and Cheddar cheese, that's fine. Trust me, once they see how much you're enjoying this delicious, crunchy, cauliflower and broccoli salad, they'll be begging for their own bowl.

SHOPPING LIST

DRESSING

¾ cup mayonnaise

½ cup sour cream

1 teaspoon cider vinegar

1 teaspoon sugar substitute

¼ teaspoon onion powder

¼ teaspoon salt

¼ teaspoon black pepper

SALAD

16 ounces frozen cauliflower
   florets, thawed (see tip)

16 ounces frozen broccoli florets, thawed

1 cup shredded Cheddar cheese

6 slices bacon, cooked and crumbled

4 green onions, thinly sliced

¼ cup shelled sunflower kernels

1 ADD all Dressing ingredients to a large mixing bowl and whisk to combine.

2 ADD the Salad ingredients into the Dressing, folding until well coated.

3 COVER and refrigerate for at least 1 hour before serving. Refrigerate overnight for even better flavor.

HELPFUL TIPS

The broccoli and cauliflower can be thawed in the fridge overnight or simply microwaved on the defrost setting for 5–7 minutes. You'd like it to be cold, but not icy.

Calories: 330 • Fat: 29g • Protein: 10.5g • Total Carbs: 8g – Fiber: 3.5g = **Net Carbs: 4.5g**

GRAIN-FREE PIZZA CRUST

YOU WON'T BELIEVE HOW IT'S MADE

Do not let the ingredients of this totally grain-free pizza crust scare you away, as the results look and (more importantly) taste spectacular. This may be made from cauliflower, but nobody has to know that and they certainly won't be able to guess!

SHOPPING LIST

1 medium head cauliflower, cut into florets

2 large eggs, beaten

½ cup shredded mozzarella cheese

¼ cup grated Parmesan cheese

1 teaspoon dried oregano

1 teaspoon dried basil

¼ teaspoon garlic powder

⅛ teaspoon black pepper

⅛ teaspoon onion powder

HELPFUL TIPS

When shopping for pizza sauce to top this crust, always be sure to check the ingredients for corn syrup or any added sugar.

1 PREHEAT oven to 350°F. Line a 10-inch pizza pan with parchment paper.

2 ADD the cauliflower florets to a food processor and blend until they are a paste-like consistency. You may need to do this in 2 batches.

3 TRANSFER the cauliflower paste to the center of a clean kitchen towel, draw up the ends, and twist the towel to remove any excess water.

4 ADD the prepared cauliflower paste to a bowl and use a fork to mix in the remaining ingredients, just until well blended.

5 PLACE the mixed dough onto the center of the prepared pan and cover with plastic wrap. Use a rolling pin to evenly spread the dough out, getting as close to the edges as you can. Discard plastic wrap.

6 BAKE the crust for 45–50 minutes, or until it begins to brown.

Cooking Pizza: Top with your favorite toppings and bake again at 350°F for 8–10 minutes, just until cheese is melted and toppings are hot.

Calories: 70 • Fat: 3.5g • Protein: 6g • Total Carbs: 3g – Fiber: 1.5g = **Net Carbs: 1.5g**

GERMAN CUCUMBER SALAD

CUCUMBERS AND ONIONS IN A CREAMY DRESSING

This cool, traditional, summer salad originated in Germany, where it is known as "gurkensalat," which is a lot of fun to say. Full of fresh, crisp, cucumbers and smooth, creamy dressing, it perfectly compliments almost any meal. It is also equally delicious straight out of the bowl, standing in the glow of the refrigerator, in the middle of the night…. So I've been told.

SHOPPING LIST

DRESSING

⅓ cup sour cream

3 tablespoons cider vinegar

2 tablespoons chopped fresh parsley

2 tablespoons sugar substitute

½ teaspoon salt

¼ teaspoon ground mustard

¼ teaspoon black pepper

SALAD

3 large cucumbers, peeled and thinly sliced

½ yellow onion, thinly sliced

3 green onions, thinly sliced

1 ADD all Dressing ingredients to a large mixing bowl and whisk to combine.

2 ADD the Salad ingredients into the Dressing, folding until well coated.

3 COVER and refrigerate for at least 2 hours before serving.

HELPFUL TIPS

The thinner you can slice the cucumbers and onions for this salad, the better. A mandolin slicer works the best for slicing the cucumbers nice and uniformly.

LUNCH

Calories: 35 • Fat: 2g • Protein: 1g • Total Carbs: 4g – Fiber: 0.5g = **Net Carbs: 3.5g**

CILANTRO LIME CHICKEN SALAD

CHUNKY CHICKEN SALAD WITH SOUTHWESTERN FLAVORS

There are so many things that could be made a bit more vibrant by adding just a dash of the American Southwest. Simple chicken salad is definitely one of those things. The bright zest of lime and the fragrant, citrus pop of cilantro help turn an old black and white standard into a Technicolor classic!

LUNCH

SHOPPING LIST

DRESSING

½ cup sour cream

¼ cup mayonnaise

Juice of 1 lime

¼ teaspoon lime zest

¼ teaspoon sugar substitute, or more to taste

¼ teaspoon ground cumin

¼ teaspoon salt

¼ teaspoon black pepper

SALAD

2 cups shredded or diced cooked chicken breast

¼ cup chopped cilantro

3 tablespoons finely diced red bell pepper

1 ADD all Dressing ingredients to a large mixing bowl and whisk to combine.

2 ADD the Salad ingredients into the Dressing, folding until well coated.

3 COVER and refrigerate for at least 1 hour before serving.

HELPFUL TIPS

For a full meal, serve a scoop of this chicken salad on a bed of lettuce with sliced avocado, diced tomato, and sliced black olives.

Calories: 185 • Fat: 12.5g • Protein: 17g • Total Carbs: 1g − Fiber: 0g = **Net Carbs: 1g**

THE "MAC" BURGER WRAP

A "BIG" FAST FOOD FAVORITE, ALL WRAPPED UP

We all know the jingle: two all-beef patties, special sauce, cheese, pickles, onions, sesame seeds, in a healthy and delicious lettuce wrap. Okay, maybe that's not EXACTLY how it goes, but I certainly like it better.

LUNCH

SHOPPING LIST

4 (¼-pound) ground beef patties

Salt and black pepper

2 slices deluxe American cheese, cut in half

4 large lettuce leaves, such as Bibb lettuce

¼ cup dill pickle slices

¼ cup thinly sliced white onion

2 teaspoons toasted sesame seeds

SPECIAL SAUCE

¼ cup mayonnaise

2 teaspoons sugar substitute

2 teaspoons tomato paste

2 teaspoons sugar-free sweet relish

1½ teaspoons white vinegar

⅛ teaspoon onion powder

1 pinch salt and black pepper

1 GENEROUSLY season the ground beef patties with salt and pepper.

2 GRILL, broil, or pan-fry the burgers over medium-high heat until your desired temperature, about 3 minutes on each side for medium doneness.

3 SLICE each burger in half to make 2 half-moon-shaped patties. Place ½ slice of American cheese in between each pair of the cut patties.

4 LAY out 4 large leaves of lettuce. Place a pair of cut burger patties with cheese atop each lettuce leaf.

5 TOP with pickles, onion, and a dollop of Special Sauce. Sprinkle with toasted sesame seeds. Roll each lettuce leaf over the filling ingredients like a burrito to finish the wraps.

Special Sauce: In a small bowl, whisk together all Special Sauce ingredients, until combined.

Toasting Sesame Seeds: Place a small skillet over medium heat. Cook the sesame seeds while constantly shaking the pan, just until seeds are lightly browned and fragrant, just 3–4 minutes.

Calories: 385 • Fat: 31g • Protein: 23.5g • Total Carbs: 2.5g – Fiber: 0.5g = **Net Carbs: 2g**

GRILLED EGGPLANT AND PEAR SALAD

WITH WALNUTS AND SMOKED GOUDA

Though at first glance they may seem at odds, eggplant and pears actually compliment each other delightfully. The soft, pleasantly bitter quality of the eggplant is balanced by the crispy sweetness of the pear. Add in smoky Gouda and the earthy crunch of walnuts, and this hearty, elegant salad will be the talk of the table.

LUNCH

SHOPPING LIST

SALAD

1 medium eggplant

1 tablespoon olive oil

Salt and black pepper

1 bag (6–10 ounces) fancy salad greens

1 large pear, cored and sliced

2 ounces smoked Gouda
  cheese, thinly sliced

¼ cup shelled walnuts

DRESSING

3 tablespoons extra virgin olive oil

2 tablespoons balsamic vinegar

1 tablespoon Dijon mustard

½ teaspoon dried rosemary

¼ teaspoon garlic powder

¼ teaspoon salt

¼ teaspoon black pepper

1 PREHEAT a grill or grill pan over medium-high heat.

2 SLICE top and bottom off eggplant and discard. Slice eggplant into 8 thick slices about ¾ inch thick. Toss eggplant slices in olive oil and lightly season with salt and pepper.

3 PLACE the eggplant slices on the hot grill and cook for 3–4 minutes on each side, until eggplant is tender. Remove from grill and let cool.

4 SPLIT the salad greens evenly between 4 serving bowls.

5 TOP the salad greens in each bowl with an equal amount of grilled eggplant, sliced pear, sliced Gouda cheese, and walnuts.

6 ADD all Dressing ingredients to a mixing bowl and whisk to combine. Drizzle over each salad before serving.

HELPFUL TIPS

Any cheese can be used in place of the smoked Gouda, though a semi-soft cheese (such as Fontina, Havarti, or Monterey Jack) is best.

Calories: 280 • Fat: 23g • Protein: 6.5g • Total Carbs: 15g – Fiber: 6g = **Net Carbs: 9g**

APPETIZERS & SNACKS

CONTENTS

BUFFALO CHICKEN STUFFED MUSHROOMS

TWO GAME DAY FAVORITES IN ONE

Forget the Wet-Naps you normally need to break out for Buffalo wings. These delicious little party-poppers will give you and your guests all the flavor you've come to love from two classic snacks, in one edible cup. Your fingers will be clean, but they might get tired from always reaching for another.

SHOPPING LIST

Nonstick cooking spray

1 pound large button mushrooms (about 16 mushrooms)

⅔ cup finely shredded cooked chicken breast (see tip)

1 large egg white, beaten

2 tablespoons minced celery

2 tablespoons unsalted butter, melted

2 tablespoons Louisiana Hot Sauce

¼ cup crumbled Gorgonzola cheese

1 PREHEAT oven to 375°F. Spray a sheet pan with nonstick cooking spray.

2 SCRUB mushrooms clean. Remove stems and discard.

3 PLACE chicken, egg white, celery, butter, and Louisiana Hot Sauce in a mixing bowl and mix well.

4 STUFF each mushroom until overflowing with the filling.

5 PLACE the stuffed mushrooms on the prepared sheet pan. Top each with a few crumbles of Gorgonzola cheese.

6 BAKE for 15 minutes, or until mushrooms are tender and filling is bubbly hot.

HELPFUL TIPS

One-half cup of any cooked chicken meat can be used in this recipe. Leftover rotisserie chicken works particularly well.

APPETIZERS

Calories: 160 • Fat: 9.5g • Protein: 15.5g • Total Carbs: 5g – Fiber: 2g = **Net Carbs: 3g**

ZUCCHINI-WRAPPED TURKEY ROLLS

LOW-CARB PINWHEELS WITH A CHIVE CHEESE SPREAD

You might think these pretty little pinwheels look too good to eat, but you'd be missing out. Fresh sliced zucchini is rolled up with lean, protein-packed turkey, and a savory cheese spread to make for an out-of-this-world appetizer. Sometimes great art is meant to be eaten.

SHOPPING LIST

2 long zucchini

4–6 large slices deli turkey,
    cut into long strips

CHEESE SPREAD

4 ounces cream cheese, softened

2 tablespoons chopped fresh chives

1 tablespoon diced pimentos, drained

½ teaspoon minced garlic

⅛ teaspoon salt

⅛ teaspoon black pepper

HELPFUL TIPS

Any deli meat, or a combination of deli meats, can be used in place of the turkey in this recipe. Adding a pinch of prepared horseradish to the Cheese Spread goes really well with roast beef.

1 CUT ends from zucchini. Slice each zucchini into at least 8 thin slices lengthwise. Using a mandolin slicer is highly recommended.

2 IN a mixing bowl, use a fork to whisk together all Cheese Spread ingredients.

3 ON a large surface, lay out all slices of zucchini. Spread a scant tablespoon of the Cheese Spread over the entire surface of each slice.

4 TOP the Cheese Spread on each zucchini with 2 long strips of deli turkey.

5 STARTING at one end of each slice, roll the zucchini up into a pinwheel. You can secure the pinwheel to prevent it from unrolling by using a dab of the cheese spread to stick the zucchini to itself, or simply serve skewered with toothpicks.

6 FOR best flavor, cover and refrigerate for 30 minutes before serving.

APPETIZERS

Calories: 145 • Fat: 10.5g • Protein: 10g • Total Carbs: 4g – Fiber: 1g = **Net Carbs: 3g**

SKEWERED GREEK SALAD STACKS

A SIMPLE, FRESH, AND ELEGANT FINGER FOOD

"If it ain't broke, don't fix it;" and there's certainly nothing broken about the fresh, classic, flavors of a Greek salad. But no one ever said, "If it ain't broke, don't put it on a skewer so it's easier to eat." So that's just what I've done with this Mediterranean favorite.

SHOPPING LIST

1 small cucumber

4 ounces feta cheese (not crumbled)

16 grape tomatoes

16 pitted Kalamata olives

2 tablespoons extra virgin olive oil

1 tablespoon red wine vinegar

Salt and black pepper

Dried oregano

HELPFUL TIPS

Fancy toothpicks make all the difference when serving simple appetizers such as this one. Check the party supply section of your grocery or big-box store for more options than you will find in the paper goods aisle.

1 CUT the cucumber into ½-inch thick discs. Cut each disc in half to make half-moon shapes.

2 CUT feta cheese into 16 small cubes.

3 ASSEMBLE 16 miniature skewers on standard toothpicks by threading a whole grape tomato, then Kalamata olive, then cube of feta, and finally a half-moon of cucumber onto each stick.

4 LAY the skewers out on a serving platter. Drizzle with olive oil and red wine vinegar. Lightly season with salt, pepper, and oregano before serving. For the best presentation, stand the skewers upright on the platter after seasoning.

Calories: 165 • Fat: 15g • Protein: 5g • Total Carbs: 4.5g – Fiber: 1g = **Net Carbs: 3.5g**

RICOTTA AND HAM STUFFED YELLOW SQUASH

TENDER BAKED SQUASH WITH A CREAMY FILLING

Few things make a better edible boat than squash. They're already stuffed with heart-healthy nutrients, so why not stuff them with more…stuff?! Rich, creamy ricotta cheese, and lean ham make an amazing meal of these humble, yellow boats. Enjoy them on their own, or serve them as a side dish alongside…other stuff!

SHOPPING LIST

Nonstick cooking spray

8 small yellow squash

Salt and black pepper

FILLING

1 cup ricotta cheese

1 large egg, beaten

1/3 cup finely diced ham

1/4 cup grated Parmesan cheese

3 tablespoons sliced green onions

1/2 teaspoon minced garlic

1/8 teaspoon salt

1/8 teaspoon black pepper

1 PREHEAT oven to 400°F. Spray a sheet pan with nonstick cooking spray.

2 SLICE ends from each squash and halve.

3 USE a sharp spoon to scoop 1/2 of the pulp out of each half of squash. Place on the prepared sheet pan and lightly season with salt and pepper.

4 IN a mixing bowl, fold together all Filling ingredients.

5 SPOON about 3 tablespoons of the ricotta filling into each of the squash halves.

6 BAKE for 15 minutes, or until squash is tender and cheese is beginning to brown. Serve immediately.

HELPFUL TIPS

These can also be made with 4 medium to large zucchini. Omit the ham to make a great side dish to serve alongside steak.

Calories: 90 • Fat: 4.5g • Protein: 7.5g • Total Carbs: 4.5g – Fiber: 1g = **Net Carbs: 3.5g**

NO-CORN CORN DOG BITES

NOBODY HAS TO KNOW THAT THEY'RE ACTUALLY LOW-CARB

I feel I need to warn you now; you may want to commit this recipe to memory. Because as soon as you break these little corn-free puppies out at a party, everyone is going to ask you how to make them. You could save yourself the trouble of repeating it by printing a few copies of the directions for your friends. Or…you can tell them about this great book you got it from.

SHOPPING LIST

Nonstick cooking spray

1 cup almond flour

¼ cup sugar substitute

1½ teaspoons baking powder

3 large eggs, beaten

⅓ cup heavy cream

1 teaspoon butter extract

¼ teaspoon vanilla extract

½ cup shredded sharp Cheddar cheese

8 hotdogs, sliced into 3
    pieces each (see tip)

HELPFUL TIPS

We buy all-beef hot dogs with "no nitrates." Regular corn dogs are made with standard hot dogs (a mixture of chicken, pork, and beef), which you can also find without nitrates. There are conflicting studies on nitrates, but our thoughts are that there's no reason to eat them when alternatives are available!

1 PREHEAT oven to 375°F. Generously spray a 24-count mini-muffin pan with nonstick cooking spray.

2 IN a large mixing bowl, combine the almond flour, sugar substitute, and baking powder.

3 ADD the eggs, heavy cream, butter extract, and vanilla extract, and whisk until completely blended into a batter.

4 FOLD the Cheddar cheese into the batter.

5 USING a tablespoon or 1-ounce ice cream scoop, place a heaping spoonful of batter into each of the prepared muffin cups.

6 STICK a piece of hotdog into the center of the batter in each muffin cup.

7 BAKE for 17–20 minutes, until the tops are golden brown. Remove from the pan while they are still hot. If they do not easily release from the pan, they need to bake for a few more minutes. Serve hot with plenty of mustard for dipping.

Calories: 245 • Fat: 11.5g • Protein: 12.5g • Total Carbs: 5.5g – Fiber: 1.5g = **Net Carbs: 4g**

JALAPEÑO POPPER BITES

MINI JALAPEÑO AND CHEESE MUFFINS

Bring these "bites" out for brunch and add a little spice to your Sunday. Or Monday night. Or holiday party. Or…anytime really. Rich, creamy ricotta and the zip of fresh jalapeño, packed into a mini-muffin popper, requires no special occasion. They ARE the occasion.

SHOPPING LIST

Nonstick cooking spray

4 large eggs

¼ cup grated Parmesan cheese

¼ cup ricotta cheese

⅓ cup shredded sharp Cheddar cheese

1 tablespoon seeded and minced fresh jalapeño (about 1 small pepper)

¼ teaspoon butter extract (see tip)

1 PREHEAT oven to 350°F and spray a 24-count mini-muffin pan with nonstick cooking spray.

2 ADD all ingredients to a large mixing bowl and whisk until combined.

3 USING a 1-ounce ice cream scoop or a heaping tablespoon, fill 18 mini-muffin cups with an equal amount of the batter. (Leave the remaining 6 mini-muffin cups empty.)

4 BAKE for 17–20 minutes, or until the tops begin to brown. Serve warm.

HELPFUL TIPS

The butter extract adds more flavor, however it can be omitted in a pinch.

APPETIZERS

Calories: 105 • Fat: 7.5g • Protein: 9g • Total Carbs: 1g − Fiber: 0g = **Net Carbs: 1g**

"EVERYTHING" SEASONED POPCORN

WITH EVERYONE'S FAVORITE BAGEL SEASONING

I know, I know, the "Everything" seasoning in this recipe isn't actually made from "everything"—and thankfully not—as I could never fit such nonsense on a single page. But instead of worrying about everything that isn't actually in "Everything," you should make this delicious snack that takes its inspiration from the seasoning on the classic "Everything" bagels.

SHOPPING LIST

SEASONING

1 tablespoon dried minced onion

1 tablespoon dried minced garlic

1 tablespoon poppy seeds

1 tablespoon sesame seeds, toasted (see method)

¾ teaspoon salt

POPCORN

3 tablespoons vegetable oil

½ cup popcorn kernels

2 tablespoons unsalted butter, melted

Toasting Sesame Seeds: Place a small skillet over medium heat. Cook the sesame seeds while constantly shaking the pan, just until seeds are lightly browned and fragrant, just 3–4 minutes.

1 COMBINE all Seasoning ingredients and set aside.

2 ADD the vegetable oil to a heavy 6-quart pot with lid. Place over high heat for 1 minute.

3 POUR popcorn kernels into the pot and cover.

4 CONSTANTLY shake the pot in a side to side motion as the popcorn pops. Once popping has slowed to more than 3 seconds between pops, remove from heat.

5 TRANSFER popped popcorn to a large serving bowl. Drizzle with melted butter and toss with the seasoning before serving.

HELPFUL TIPS

For a finer seasoning that better sticks to the popcorn, simply place the whole seasoning mix into a spice or coffee grinder and pulse until the large pieces of garlic and onion are broken up.

APPETIZERS

Calories: 125 • Fat: 9.5g • Protein: 2g • Total Carbs: 10.5g – Fiber: 2.5g = **Net Carbs: 8g**

GUACAMOLE STUFFED DEVILED EGGS

I DO, I LIKE THEM, SAM-I-AM! THESE GREEN EGGS, WITHOUT THE HAM

This colorful, eye-catching variation on a go-to snack is a sure-fire conversation starter. The fact that these little devils are filled with heart-healthy avocado might even make you question their mischievous name. But, "Angelic Eggs" just doesn't have the same ring to it.

SHOPPING LIST

8 large hard-boiled eggs, peeled

1 Hass avocado, pitted and peeled

Juice of ½ lime

2 tablespoons chopped fresh cilantro

1 tablespoon minced red onion

1 clove garlic, minced

¼ teaspoon salt

⅛ teaspoon black pepper

Chili powder, for garnish

Sliced black olives, for garnish

1 CUT eggs in half lengthwise and remove yolks. Transfer the egg whites to a serving platter.

2 PLACE 4 of the yolks in a large mixing bowl. Discard remaining yolks.

3 ADD all remaining ingredients, except garnishes, to the mixing bowl and use a heavy fork to mash into a smooth guacamole.

4 USE a pastry bag with a large opening to pipe the guacamole into each egg white half.

5 SPRINKLE the deviled eggs lightly with chili powder and top each with a sliced black olive, for garnish.

HELPFUL TIPS

For an extra smooth and creamy filling, simply use a food processor to purée the egg yolks and guacamole ingredients.

Calories: 105 • Fat: 8g • Protein: 7g • Total Carbs: 2.5g – Fiber: 0.5g = **Net Carbs: 2g**

CARAMELIZED ONION DIP

TRUE FRENCH ONION DIP WITH A WHOLE LOT OF REAL ONIONS

The list of things I would dunk in this delicious dip would be longer than this entire book. I might even dip the book itself, if no one was looking! Well, maybe not, but that's how good this creamy dip with a savory hit of caramelized onions really is.

APPETIZERS

SHOPPING LIST

1 tablespoon olive oil

1 yellow onion, thinly sliced

2 teaspoons balsamic vinegar

1 teaspoon sugar substitute

16 ounces sour cream

¼ cup mayonnaise

1 teaspoon beef base (see tip)

1 teaspoon balsamic vinegar

1 teaspoon minced garlic

1 teaspoon onion powder

¼ teaspoon salt

¼ teaspoon black pepper

1 HEAT the olive oil in a large skillet over medium heat.

2 PLACE the sliced onion in the skillet and cook, stirring occasionally, until well caramelized, about 15 minutes.

3 STIR balsamic vinegar and sugar substitute into the onion. Cook for 1 additional minute. Let cool at least 5 minutes.

4 IN a large mixing bowl, fold the onion mixture together with remaining ingredients.

5 COVER and refrigerate for at least 2 hours before serving. Season with additional salt or sugar substitute to taste.

HELPFUL TIPS

Beef base (sold in small jars by brands such as Better Than Bouillon) is usually located near the bouillon cubes in the grocery store.

Calories: 185 · Fat: 18.5g · Protein: 2g · Total Carbs: 3.5g – Fiber: 0g = **Net Carbs: 3.5g**

GREEK MEATBALLS

BAKED MEATBALLS STUFFED WITH FETA AND ROASTED RED PEPPERS

The hardest part about serving these amazing Mediterranean meatballs to your guests is…having to give them away. But since the recipe is inspired by Greece, its customs should inspire you as well: the Greeks believe a meal should always be enjoyed with friends. So go ahead…let go of the tray.

SHOPPING LIST

Nonstick cooking spray

1 pound lean ground beef

1 large egg, beaten

½ cup crumbled feta cheese

¼ cup finely diced roasted red pepper

1 tablespoon chopped fresh mint

1½ teaspoons minced garlic

1 teaspoon lemon juice

1 teaspoon dried oregano

½ teaspoon lemon zest

½ teaspoon salt

¼ teaspoon black pepper

1 PREHEAT oven to 375°F. Spray a sheet pan with nonstick cooking spray.

2 COMBINE ground beef and all remaining ingredients in a large mixing bowl.

3 USE your hands to mix and then form the ground beef mixture into golf ball-sized meatballs. Transfer to the prepared sheet pan.

4 BAKE for 20 minutes, or until slicing into a meatball reveals no pink. Serve stuck with toothpicks.

HELPFUL TIPS

These are very good when served alongside a simple dipping sauce made from ½ cup of no-sugar-added ketchup mixed with 1 tablespoon chopped fresh mint, 1 teaspoon lemon zest, and ¼ teaspoon garlic powder.

APPETIZERS

Calories: 160 • Fat: 9g • Protein: 18.5g • Total Carbs: 1g − Fiber: 0g = **Net Carbs: 1g**

PIMENTO CHEESE SPREAD

JUST LIKE MY "GRAM" USED TO MAKE

Gram used to make this delicious cheese spread during the holidays, and it was one of my absolute favorites. Place it as the centerpiece of a colorful tray of crudités and spread a little holiday cheer of your own.

SHOPPING LIST

8 ounces shredded sharp Cheddar cheese

½ cup mayonnaise

1 (4-ounce) jar diced pimentos, drained

1 tablespoon Dijon mustard

½ teaspoon paprika

¼ teaspoon ground mustard

¼ teaspoon black pepper

2 tablespoons water

Salt

1 COMBINE all ingredients, except water and salt, in a microwave-safe mixing bowl.

2 MICROWAVE in 20-second intervals, stirring each time, just until cheese has mostly melted into the mayonnaise. Just 80–100 seconds is all you need, as you want the dip melted, but not bubbling hot.

3 ONCE melted, let cool for 2 minutes before whisking 2 tablespoons of water into the dip. Season with salt to taste.

4 SERVE warm or chilled. For best flavor, cover and refrigerate overnight. Stir well before serving spread over sliced fresh vegetables.

HELPFUL TIPS

Two tablespoons of finely diced jalapeño pepper will add more of a peppery kick to this dip.

APPETIZERS

Calories: 210 • Fat: 19.5g • Protein: 7.5g • Total Carbs: 1.5g − Fiber: 0g = **Net Carbs: 1.5g**

COCOA ROASTED PEANUTS

THE COZY FEELING YOU GET FROM HOT COCOA...ON A PEANUT

These cocoa-coated legumes are almost too good to be true. Each time you reach for a few more you'll get that feeling like you've been caught with your hand in the cookie jar. But don't worry, these protein-packed peanuts are a healthy, filling snack. They just happen to taste like candy.

SHOPPING LIST

1 (16-ounce) can salted cocktail peanuts

1 large egg white, beaten

¾ teaspoon vanilla extract

½ cup sugar substitute

2½ tablespoons cocoa powder

HELPFUL TIPS

These make a great holiday gift when packaged in a decorative candy bag, jar, or keepsake tin.

1 PREHEAT oven to 300°F. Line a sheet pan with parchment paper.

2 IN a large mixing bowl, toss the peanuts in the egg white and vanilla extract.

3 IN a small bowl, combine sugar substitute and cocoa powder.

4 ADD ½ of the cocoa powder mixture to the peanuts and toss until all peanuts are evenly coated.

5 SPREAD the coated peanuts out onto the prepared sheet pan. Sprinkle the remaining ½ of the cocoa powder mixture over top all.

6 BAKE for 20 minutes, stirring halfway through. Let cool for 5 minutes before serving.

APPETIZERS

Calories: 235 • Fat: 19g • Protein: 10g • Total Carbs: 8g – Fiber: 3g = **Net Carbs: 5g**

CAN'T BELIEVE IT'S KALE CHIPS

CRUNCHY BAKED KALE CHIPS YOU CAN'T RESIST

The amount of essential vitamins and minerals kale has to offer cannot be understated. Any creative way to work more kale into your diet should be taken advantage of. One of the easiest ways to do that is with this crispy, delicious snack. All hail the kale! King/Queen of the Superfoods!

SHOPPING LIST

1 bunch kale

1 tablespoon olive oil

¼ teaspoon salt

¼ teaspoon black pepper

⅛ teaspoon onion powder

⅛ teaspoon garlic powder

HELPFUL TIPS

The kale shrinks considerably as it bakes, so do not be afraid to overcrowd the sheet pan.

1 PREHEAT oven to 350°F. Line a sheet pan with parchment paper.

2 RINSE kale and pat dry with paper towels. Remove leaves from stems and tear into bite-sized pieces. Discard stems.

3 IN a large mixing bowl, toss kale with all remaining ingredients, evenly coating with the olive oil and spices.

4 ARRANGE the coated kale on the prepared sheet pan in a single layer.

5 BAKE for 15 minutes, or until the edges of the leaves have browned and chips are crisp. Serve immediately.

APPETIZERS

Calories: 65 • Fat: 3.5g • Protein: 2g • Total Carbs: 7g − Fiber: 1g = **Net Carbs: 6g**

ALBACORE TUNA CAKES

AN INEXPENSIVE AND EASY ALTERNATIVE TO CRAB CAKES

Easier on the wallet, and packing more protein (pound for pound) than crab, these savory little tuna patties are perfect for parties, or even over a light, leafy salad for lunch.

SHOPPING LIST

2 large eggs

2 tablespoons ground flax seed

1 tablespoon baking powder

1 tablespoon mayonnaise

1 tablespoon lemon juice

2 teaspoons Dijon mustard

1/4 teaspoon salt

1/8 teaspoon black pepper

15 ounces canned albacore
    white tuna, drained

2 tablespoons finely diced red bell pepper

2 tablespoons chopped chives

2 tablespoons vegetable oil, divided

Lemon wedges, for garnish

HELPFUL TIPS

Make a simple tartar sauce to serve alongside these by combining 1/4 cup of mayonnaise, 2 tablespoons of sugar-free sweet pickle relish, and a dash of lemon juice.

1 IN a large mixing bowl, whisk together the eggs, flax seed, baking powder, mayonnaise, lemon juice, Dijon mustard, salt, and pepper.

2 FOLD the tuna, bell pepper, and chives into the egg mixture until all is combined into a batter. The batter may be somewhat loose, but the egg will firm up as it cooks.

3 HEAT 1 tablespoon of the vegetable oil in a large skillet over medium-high heat.

4 CAREFULLY spoon 6 rounded tablespoons of the batter (about 1/2 of the batter) into the hot skillet to create silver dollar-sized tuna cakes.

5 COOK the tuna cakes until the bottom is firm, about 2 minutes. Flip and cook for 1 additional minute on the opposite side, or until cakes are firm throughout and beginning to brown.

6 REPEAT with the remaining tablespoon of vegetable oil and remaining 6 tablespoons of batter to make a total of 12 tuna cakes. Serve immediately, garnished with fresh lemon wedges, if desired.

APPETIZERS

Calories: 170 • Fat: 9.5g • Protein: 19g • Total Carbs: 2g – Fiber: 1g = **Net Carbs: 1g**

PORTABELLA PIZZAS

ROASTED MUSHROOM PIES WITH PEPPERONI AND PEPPERS

So far in this book, we've learned that squash make great boats, and that tomatoes make perfect cups. Now, the mighty, meaty portabella makes a case to be taken seriously as…a pizza crust? I think you'll find it makes a compellingly tasty argument. Whip these little portabella-pepperoni-pizza caps up, and the verdict will be unanimous: the defendant is delicious as charged!

SHOPPING LIST

Nonstick cooking spray

4 portabella mushroom caps, stems removed

1 tablespoon olive oil

Salt and black pepper

⅓ cup no-sugar-added pizza or spaghetti sauce

⅔ cup shredded mozzarella cheese

12 slices pepperoni

¼ cup diced green bell pepper

Italian seasoning

HELPFUL TIPS

It should go without saying that any of your favorite pizza toppings can be substituted in place of the pepperoni and green bell peppers.

1 PREHEAT oven to 400°F. Spray a sheet pan with nonstick cooking spray.

2 RUB mushrooms with olive oil and transfer to the prepared sheet pan. Lightly season with salt and pepper.

3 BAKE for 20 minutes, flipping halfway through.

4 FILL each mushroom cap with an equal amount of the pizza sauce. Top each with an equal amount of the mozzarella cheese.

5 ARRANGE 3 slices of pepperoni on top of the cheese and then sprinkle with diced bell pepper. Lightly season all with Italian seasoning.

6 SET broiler to high. Broil the topped pizzas for 2–3 minutes, or until cheese is bubbly hot and pepperoni is crisp. Serve immediately.

APPETIZERS

Calories: 190 • Fat: 14g • Protein: 11g • Total Carbs: 5.5g – Fiber: 1.5g = **Net Carbs: 4g**

CHESAPEAKE CHICKEN WINGS

CRISPY BAKED CHICKEN WINGS WITH OLD BAY SEASONING

Everyone loves crispy chicken wings; and people have been putting Old Bay Seasoning on just about anything edible since it was invented in Baltimore in 1939. I don't even know why I'm still writing this. Once you read "chicken wings" and "Old Bay" you probably stopped reading, and started cooking. I completely understand.

SHOPPING LIST

3 pounds fresh chicken wings, drum and wing separated

2 tablespoons olive oil

1 tablespoon unsalted butter, melted

1 tablespoon Old Bay Seasoning

Juice of ½ lemon

1 teaspoon baking powder

¼ teaspoon black pepper

1 PREHEAT oven to 375°F. Line a sheet pan with aluminum foil.

2 IN a large mixing bowl, toss the chicken wings with all remaining ingredients.

3 SPREAD the wings out onto the prepared sheet pan, arranging in a single layer.

4 BAKE for 50 minutes, or until slicing into the thickest drum reveals no pink. Serve immediately.

HELPFUL TIPS

The baking powder in this recipe is a secret ingredient that helps the skin bake up crisp without deep frying. It raises the pH level in the skin, causing it to brown. This is the same reason you add baking *soda* to pancakes or cookies, however baking *powder* works best with meat.

APPETIZERS

Calories: 375 • Fat: 30g • Protein: 25.5g • Total Carbs: 0.5g − Fiber: 0g = **Net Carbs: 0.5g**

POULTRY

CONTENTS

CHICKEN PRIMAVERA SAUTÉ

WITH SUMMER VEGETABLES AND BASIL

A simple sauté of chicken tenderloins and colorful vegetables, this mélange of Italian ingredients was actually created in… Canada! How such a summery dish came out of The Great White North, I do not know, but thankfully I only need to know how to cook it.

SHOPPING LIST

2 tablespoons extra virgin olive oil

1 pound chicken tenderloins, sliced into 1-inch lengths

¼ cup thinly sliced red onion

2 yellow squash, sliced

1 large zucchini, sliced

½ red bell pepper, thinly sliced

¼ cup chicken broth or stock

½ teaspoon Italian seasoning

¼ teaspoon black pepper

⅛ teaspoon salt

⅓ cup grated Parmesan cheese

2 tablespoons chopped fresh basil

1 HEAT oil in a large skillet over high heat, until nearly smoking hot.

2 ADD the chicken tenderloins and onion to the hot skillet. Sauté until chicken is lightly browned, about 4 minutes.

3 REDUCE heat to medium-high. Add the squash, zucchini, bell pepper, chicken broth, Italian seasoning, pepper, and salt to the skillet.

4 SAUTÉ for 5 minutes, or until vegetables are crisp-tender.

5 REMOVE from heat and stir in Parmesan cheese and basil before serving.

HELPFUL TIPS

Any combination of vegetables can be used in this sauté. When using green vegetables like broccoli or green beans, it is recommended that you lightly steam them before adding to the skillet. Or simply use thawed frozen vegetables.

POULTRY

Calories: 250 • Fat: 11.5g • Protein: 32g • Total Carbs: 7.5g − Fiber: 2.5g = **Net Carbs: 5g**

ARUGULA PESTO CHICKEN

BONELESS CHICKEN BREASTS WITH ARUGULA AND WALNUT PESTO

While pesto is typically made with pine nuts and basil, this recipe uses peppery fresh arugula and earthy walnuts in their place. While it may not be traditional, this new combination brings unique and delicious flavors to the pesto-party, whether "tradition" invited them or not.

SHOPPING LIST

4 boneless, skinless chicken breasts

ARUGULA PESTO

2 packed cups arugula

¼ cup olive oil

¼ cup chopped walnuts, lightly toasted

¼ cup grated Parmesan cheese

1 clove garlic, peeled

Juice of ½ lemon

¼ teaspoon salt

¼ teaspoon black pepper

Toasting Walnuts: Place on a sheet pan lined with parchment paper. Bake in a 375°F oven for 6 minutes, just until fragrant.

1 PREHEAT oven to 375°F.

2 ADD all Arugula Pesto ingredients to a food processor and pulse until mostly smooth.

3 IN a mixing bowl, toss chicken breasts in the Arugula Pesto to fully coat. Transfer coated chicken to a sheet pan and scrape any remaining pesto from the bowl to spread over top of each chicken breast.

4 BAKE for 25–30 minutes, or until slicing into the thickest piece of chicken reveals no pink. Serve immediately.

HELPFUL TIPS

Pine nuts are typically used in pesto sauce and can be substituted for the walnuts in this recipe. They take 8–10 minutes to toast in a 375°F oven.

POULTRY

Calories: 430 • Fat: 21.5g • Protein: 57g • Total Carbs: 1.5g – Fiber: 0.5g = **Net Carbs: 1g**

PROSCIUTTO WRAPPED CHICKEN BREASTS

A RESTAURANT-QUALITY CHICKEN DISH MADE EASY

The succulent, salty taste of prosciutto in this dish adds a little "mean" to the chicken breast's "lean." Add in the light, spicy, zip of Dijon, and traditional Italian spices, and you've got the perfect protein portion for a lean AND mean dinner to die for.

SHOPPING LIST

4 boneless, skinless chicken breasts

2 tablespoons olive oil, divided

1 tablespoon Dijon mustard

½ teaspoon minced garlic

½ teaspoon red wine vinegar

¼ teaspoon dried oregano

¼ teaspoon black pepper

8 slices prosciutto

HELPFUL TIPS

For even more Italian flavors, place 2 whole leaves of fresh basil over top of each chicken breast before you wrap it with the prosciutto.

1 PREHEAT oven to 375°F.

2 IN a large mixing bowl, toss chicken with 1 tablespoon of the olive oil, Dijon mustard, garlic, vinegar, oregano, and pepper. Make sure each breast is evenly coated.

3 LAY out 2 slices of the prosciutto so that they are slightly overlapping each other.

4 PLACE a coated chicken breast over top of the prosciutto and then wrap the prosciutto around the chicken, pressing down to allow it to stick to the meat. Repeat with the remaining 6 slices of prosciutto and 3 chicken breasts.

5 HEAT the remaining tablespoon of olive oil in a large oven-proof skillet over medium-high heat.

6 ADD the wrapped chicken breasts to the skillet and cook for 4 minutes on each side, or until prosciutto is crispy.

7 TRANSFER the skillet to the oven and bake for 10–15 minutes, just until slicing into the thickest chicken breast reveals no pink.

POULTRY

Calories: 335 • Fat: 10g • Protein: 56.5g • Total Carbs: 0.5g − Fiber: 0g = **Net Carbs: 0.5g**

ROASTED CURRY CHICKEN

TENDER CHICKEN LEG QUARTERS WITH A BOLD BLEND OF SPICES

Chicken leg quarters are one of the most under-appreciated (and inexpensive) proteins you can pick up at any grocery store. The dark meat of the thigh and leg cooks up as moist as chicken gets, and with plenty of crispy skin over top of it. In this recipe, the bold, but not too spicy, flavors of curry are roasted into the chicken for a leg up on the dinner competition.

SHOPPING LIST

4 chicken leg quarters

2 tablespoons vegetable oil

2 teaspoons curry powder

¼ teaspoon ground cumin

¼ teaspoon allspice

½ teaspoon salt

HELPFUL TIPS

I like to add a teaspoon of sugar substitute to the spice mixture, just to add a bit of sweetness to all of the strong flavors.

1 PREHEAT oven to 375°F.

2 IN a large mixing bowl, toss chicken leg quarters in all remaining ingredients, evenly coating each piece.

3 TRANSFER the coated leg quarters to a sheet pan.

4 BAKE for 50–55 minutes, or until a meat thermometer inserted into the thickest part registers 175°F.

5 LET rest for 5 minutes before serving.

POULTRY

Calories: 355 • Fat: 26.5g • Protein: 29g • Total Carbs: 0.5g − Fiber: 0g = **Net Carbs: 0.5g**

CHICKEN THIGH OSSO BUCO

WITH TRADITIONAL LEMON ZEST AND PARSLEY "GREMOLATA"

This is my take on a classic that comes straight from the top of the boot; Milan, Italy. Typically made with veal shank, the substitution of chicken thighs makes this a whole lot less expensive, without sacrificing any of those robust Italian flavors. Top with a traditional, chopped-parsley and lemon gremolata for the full flavors of a true favorite.

SHOPPING LIST

1 tablespoon olive oil

2 pounds chicken thighs

Salt and black pepper

Paprika

2 stalks celery, diced

¼ cup diced red onion

2 cloves garlic, smashed

⅓ cup dry red wine

1 (14.5-ounce) can diced tomatoes, with liquid

1 tablespoon tomato paste

1¼ teaspoons Italian seasoning

¼ teaspoon salt

¼ teaspoon black pepper

GREMOLATA

¼ cup fresh parsley, finely chopped

Zest of 1 lemon

1 teaspoon minced garlic

Salt and black pepper

1 HEAT oil in a large skillet or Dutch oven over medium-high heat.

2 GENEROUSLY season chicken with salt, pepper, and paprika.

3 ADD chicken to the skillet and cook on both sides until the skin is well browned, about 8 minutes. Remove chicken and set aside.

4 ADD celery, onion, and garlic to the skillet and sauté 2 minutes.

5 ADD the red wine, diced tomatoes with liquid, tomato paste, Italian seasoning, salt, and pepper to the skillet. Stir to combine.

6 RETURN chicken to the skillet, lower heat to a simmer, and cover.

7 LET simmer 40 minutes before serving topped with the Gremolata.

Preparing the Gremolata: Use a fork to mix all Gremolata ingredients, seasoning to taste with salt and pepper.

HELPFUL TIPS

The Gremolata in this recipe also makes a great topping for grilled or sautéed chicken, pork, seafood, or even vegetables.

POULTRY

Calories: 510 • Fat: 35g • Protein: 40g • Total Carbs: 5.5g – Fiber: 1.5g = **Net Carbs: 4g**

MUSHROOM AND SAGE STUFFED CHICKEN

CHICKEN BREAST ROULADES WITH A CHEESY MUSHROOM STUFFING

The earthy mushroom stuffing rolled into these chicken breast pinwheels gets a bit of brightness from fragrant fresh sage. The grated Parmesan cheese adds… Well, everything is just better with cheese!

POULTRY

SHOPPING LIST

CHICKEN

4 boneless, skinless chicken breasts

Salt and black pepper

Dried thyme

STUFFING

1 tablespoon unsalted butter

4 ounces baby bella mushrooms, finely chopped

2 tablespoons minced red onion

1 teaspoon minced garlic

6 leaves fresh sage, chopped

⅛ teaspoon salt

⅛ teaspoon black pepper

¼ cup grated Parmesan cheese

HELPFUL TIPS

For a nicely browned exterior on the chicken, roll the roulades in 1 tablespoon of melted butter before baking.

1 PREHEAT oven to 400°F. Line a sheet pan with parchment paper.

2 USING a meat mallet, pound the chicken breasts out until about ⅓-inch thick at all parts. Season both sides of each breast with salt, pepper, and thyme.

3 START the Stuffing by heating butter in a skillet over medium-high heat.

4 ADD the mushrooms, onion, garlic, sage, salt, and pepper to the skillet and sauté until mushrooms are tender, about 5 minutes. Drain well of excess liquid, pressing to drain additional liquid.

5 FOLD Parmesan cheese into the drained Stuffing mixture.

6 SPREAD a large dollop of the Stuffing over top one end of each pounded chicken breast, spreading to cover only the bottom ⅓ of the meat.

7 TIGHTLY roll each chicken breast up, starting on the short end, until chicken is overlapping and you have long roulades. Use toothpicks or tie with baking twine to ensure they keep their shape.

8 BAKE for 22–25 minutes, or until slicing into the largest roulade reveals no pink. Let cool for 5 minutes before serving.

Calories: 305 • Fat: 7g • Protein: 56g • Total Carbs: 2g – Fiber: 0.5g = **Net Carbs: 1.5g**

CHICKEN WITH CAJUN CREAM SAUCE

TENDERLOINS WITH A KICKIN' CREOLE-INSPIRED SAUCE

You don't have to dodge Mardi Gras floats on Bourbon Street to enjoy this celebration of Creole flavors. Cayenne pepper adds a spicy kick to the Chicken, but it's nothing that a flavorful and creamy sauce can't calm down. For the full experience, blast some zydeco music throughout your kitchen as you cook…as long as you cook when no one is looking.

SHOPPING LIST

CAJUN SEASONING

1 teaspoon paprika

½ teaspoon salt

½ teaspoon black pepper

½ teaspoon dried thyme

¼ teaspoon cayenne pepper

CHICKEN

1 tablespoon vegetable oil

1½ pounds chicken tenderloins

¼ cup dry white wine

½ cup heavy cream

1 tablespoon tomato paste

HELPFUL TIPS

This has a nice kick to it. You can make it less spicy by reducing the cayenne pepper from ¼ teaspoon to a very small pinch.

1 IN a small bowl, combine all Cajun Seasoning ingredients.

2 HEAT oil in a large skillet over medium-high heat, until nearly smoking hot.

3 Toss chicken tenderloins in ¾ of the Cajun Seasoning, reserving the remainder to season the sauce.

4 ADD seasoned tenderloins to the hot skillet and brown well, about 2 minutes on each side.

5 DEGLAZE the skillet with the white wine, scraping any seasonings from the bottom of the skillet.

6 ADD the remaining Cajun Seasoning, heavy cream, and tomato paste to the skillet and bring up to a simmer. Reduce heat to low and let simmer for 3 minutes.

7 REMOVE from heat and let cool for 3 minutes. Serve chicken tenders smothered in the sauce from the pan.

POULTRY

Calories: 240 • Fat: 10g • Protein: 35g • Total Carbs: 1.5g − Fiber: 0g = **Net Carbs: 1.5g**

BRINED TURKEY BREAST

THE SECRET TO A TENDER AND MOIST TURKEY BREAST

Ditch the dry turkey and bring on the brine! By marinating this turkey breast in a brine before roasting, you allow more moisture to make its way into the meat through the miracle of osmosis. I'm sure you've heard people jokingly use the term "osmosis," however, that last sentence was not a joke; brining actually uses osmosis to circulate water out and then back into the turkey, bringing along additional flavors in the process!

SHOPPING LIST

BRINE

1 cup kosher salt

1 teaspoon dried thyme

½ teaspoon dried rosemary

½ teaspoon ground sage

½ teaspoon black pepper

TURKEY

1 (5–7 pound) bone-in turkey breast

4 tablespoons unsalted butter

Dried thyme

Dried rosemary

Paprika

Black pepper

HELPFUL TIPS

For a truly moist turkey breast, you've got to use a meat thermometer to check for doneness. An electronic probe thermometer is best, as you can leave it in the meat and set an alarm to go off at 165°F.

1 IN a large stock pot, whisk all brine ingredients into 1 gallon of water, whisking until salt has dissolved.

2 LOWER turkey into the brine and top with a heavy bowl or dish to keep it from floating above the water line.

3 COVER and refrigerate overnight.

4 PREHEAT oven to 325°F.

5 REMOVE turkey from brine. Rinse well and pat skin dry with paper towels. Place into a roasting pan.

6 DOT the surface of the turkey breast with dollops of butter. Season skin with thyme, rosemary, paprika, and pepper.

7 BAKE for 2–2½ hours, until internal temperature reaches 165°F when measured at the thickest part.

8 LET rest for 10 minutes before carving.

POULTRY

Calories: 250 • Fat: 9g • Protein: 40g • Total Carbs: 0g – Fiber: 0g = **Net Carbs: 0g**

OVEN "SMOKED" TURKEY LEGS

A CARNIVAL FAVORITE, MADE IN YOUR KITCHEN

We've all carried around a caveman-club of a turkey leg at a carnival or amusement park. They're moist, tender, and mysteriously smoked in a complicated process that is nearly impossible to replicate indoors. I say "nearly" because this recipe emulates those smokehouse flavors in your own kitchen through the use of a few clever ingredients.

POULTRY

SHOPPING LIST

2 large turkey legs

RUB

3 tablespoons unsalted butter, softened

1 tablespoon smoked paprika

½ teaspoon salt

¼ teaspoon black pepper

¼ teaspoon liquid smoke (see tip)

HELPFUL TIPS

Liquid smoke can be omitted, as there is plenty of smoke flavor in the paprika. I like to use both, as they add two distinctly different smoke flavors that combine very well.

1 USING a fork, whisk together all Rub ingredients, until fully combined.

2 KNEAD the rub over the entire surface of each turkey leg.

3 COVER and refrigerate for at least 2 hours. Overnight is best.

4 PREHEAT oven to 350°F. Line a sheet pan with aluminum foil.

5 PLACE turkey legs on the prepared sheet pan. Bake for 60–80 minutes, or until a meat thermometer inserted into the thickest part registers 175°F.

6 LET rest for 10 minutes before serving.

Calories: 375 • Fat: 22.5g • Protein: 40g • Total Carbs: 1g − Fiber: 0.5g = **Net Carbs: 0.5g**

LEMON AND ROSEMARY CHICKEN THIGHS

CLASSIC FLAVORS, MARINATED FOR MAXIMUM IMPACT

This essential chicken recipe gives you the classic flavors of lemon and rosemary that truly makes poultry sing. Maybe not TRULY sing. Okay, now I can't get the vision of a chicken singing and dancing out of my head.

SHOPPING LIST

1½ pounds boneless, skinless chicken thighs

3 tablespoons olive oil

Juice of ½ lemon

1 teaspoon lemon zest

1 teaspoon minced garlic

1 teaspoon dried rosemary

½ teaspoon salt

¼ teaspoon black pepper

Fresh rosemary sprigs

HELPFUL TIPS

This can also be made with chicken breasts in place of the thighs by lowering the oven temperature to 375°F.

1 PLACE chicken thighs in a food storage container.

2 WHISK together all remaining ingredients, except fresh rosemary sprigs, to create a small amount of marinade.

3 ADD the marinade to the chicken and toss to thoroughly coat each thigh. Cover and refrigerate for 1 hour.

4 PREHEAT oven to 400°F.

5 PLACE the marinated chicken thighs on a sheet pan and top each with a small sprig of fresh rosemary.

6 BAKE for 25–30 minutes, or until cutting into the largest thigh reveals juices that run clear.

POULTRY

Calories: 285 • Fat: 17g • Protein: 33g • Total Carbs: 0.5g – Fiber: 0g = **Net Carbs: 0.5g**

KUNG PAO CHICKEN

SPICY CHICKEN STIR-FRY WITH PEANUTS

"Kung Pao" translates to "Palace Guardian," but a dish as delicious as this one would only attract more and more people to that palace. That said, this recipe absolutely packs a powerful, peppery punch that isn't for the faint of heart.

SHOPPING LIST

2 tablespoons vegetable oil

1 pound boneless, skinless chicken thighs, cut into ¾-inch chunks

1 red bell pepper, thinly sliced

3 stalks celery, thinly sliced

2 teaspoons minced garlic

2 teaspoons minced fresh ginger

3 tablespoons soy sauce

1 tablespoon sugar substitute

2 teaspoons cider vinegar

¾ teaspoon crushed red pepper flakes

¼ teaspoon black pepper

¼ cup roasted cocktail peanuts

6 green onions, cut into 1-inch lengths

1 teaspoon sesame oil

1 HEAT oil in a large skillet over high heat, until nearly smoking hot.

2 ADD the chunks of chicken thigh to the hot skillet. Sauté until golden brown, about 5 minutes.

3 REDUCE heat to medium-high. Add the bell pepper, celery, garlic, and ginger to the skillet and sauté for 3 minutes.

4 ADD soy sauce, sugar substitute, cider vinegar, red pepper flakes, and pepper to the skillet and continue sautéing for 4 minutes, or until bell pepper is tender.

5 STIR peanuts and green onions into the skillet and sauté for just 1 additional minute.

6 REMOVE from heat and stir in sesame oil before serving.

HELPFUL TIPS

This is typically made with dried red chili peppers, not red pepper flakes. Four whole dried Arbol chilies can be used. These are usually sold in the Latin food aisle.

POULTRY

Calories: 320 • Fat: 16.5g • Protein: 35g • Total Carbs: 6g − Fiber: 1.5g = **Net Carbs: 4.5g**

MEDITERRANEAN CHICKEN BAKE

WITH ZUCCHINI, BELL PEPPER, FETA CHEESE, AND BALSAMIC

This one-dish casserole cooks boneless chicken breasts atop a bed of colorful, flavorful, and nutrient-rich zucchini, bell pepper, and onion. A drizzle of balsamic vinegar adds a sweet bite to the finished dish, while crumbled feta cheese adds cream and salt to cut through the acidity.

SHOPPING LIST

3 zucchini, sliced

1 red bell pepper, sliced

½ yellow onion, thinly sliced

4 boneless, skinless chicken breasts

2½ tablespoons olive oil

1½ teaspoons minced garlic

1 teaspoon dried oregano

¼ teaspoon dried rosemary

¼ teaspoon onion powder

¼ teaspoon salt

¼ teaspoon black pepper

½ cup crumbled feta cheese

2 tablespoons balsamic vinegar

1 PREHEAT oven to 375°F.

2 LAYER the sliced zucchini, bell pepper, and onion in a large baking or roasting dish. Place the chicken breasts atop the vegetables.

3 IN a small mixing bowl, whisk together olive oil, garlic, oregano, rosemary, onion powder, salt, and pepper. Drizzle over the chicken and vegetables in the baking dish.

4 BAKE for 35–40 minutes, or until cutting into the thickest piece of chicken reveals no pink.

5 SPRINKLE with crumbled feta and drizzle with balsamic vinegar before serving.

HELPFUL TIPS

For the best presentation, slice each chicken breast into 6–8 slices after baking. Place back atop the vegetables and add the feta and balsamic drizzle.

POULTRY

Calories: 405 • Fat: 15g • Protein: 57g • Total Carbs: 9g − Fiber: 2.5g = **Net Carbs: 6.5g**

FRESH MEX CHICKEN BREASTS

WITH AVOCADO SALSA

We're grilling south of the border in this refreshing and flavorful chicken entrada (that's how you say entrée down here). Topped with a quick and easy salsa that includes both fresh tomato and chunks of avocado, this recipe is muy bueno!

SHOPPING LIST

4 boneless, skinless chicken breasts

1 tablespoon olive oil

2 tablespoons chopped fresh cilantro

½ teaspoon minced garlic

¼ teaspoon ground cumin

½ teaspoon salt

½ teaspoon black pepper

AVOCADO SALSA

1 tomato, diced

½ Hass avocado, pitted, peeled, and small chopped

2 tablespoons finely diced red onion

2 tablespoons chopped fresh cilantro

1 tablespoon finely diced jalapeño pepper

Juice of 1 lime

Salt and black pepper

1 IN a large mixing bowl, toss chicken breasts with olive oil, cilantro, garlic, cumin, salt, and pepper. Let set as you prepare the salsa.

2 IN a mixing bowl, gently fold together all Avocado Salsa ingredients. Season to taste with salt and pepper. Set aside.

3 GENEROUSLY oil a grill or grill pan and preheat on high heat.

4 PLACE seasoned chicken breasts on grill and cook for 8–10 minutes on each side, or until slicing into the thickest part reveals no pink.

5 SERVE each chicken breast topped with the Avocado Salsa.

HELPFUL TIPS

To bake the chicken breasts in place of grilling, preheat the oven to 375°F. Place seasoned chicken on a sheet pan and bake for 25–30 minutes, or until slicing into the thickest piece reveals no pink.

POULTRY

Calories: 310 • Fat: 8.5g • Protein: 53g • Total Carbs: 3.5g – Fiber: 1g = **Net Carbs: 2.5g**

SPINACH DIP STUFFED CHICKEN

A PROTEIN-PACKED WAY TO ENJOY A FAVORITE DIP

Whoever dubbed Spinach Dip a "dip" should have broadened their horizons! That creamy concoction of cheese and spinach with the narrow-minded name makes the perfect filling for lean chicken breasts in this elegant roulade recipe.

SHOPPING LIST

CHICKEN

4 boneless, skinless chicken breasts

Salt and black pepper

Paprika

STUFFING

½ cup frozen chopped spinach, thawed

4 ounces cream cheese, softened

1 large egg white

3 tablespoons grated Parmesan cheese

1 tablespoon finely diced red bell pepper

¼ teaspoon Worcestershire sauce

¼ teaspoon garlic powder

¼ teaspoon onion powder

¼ teaspoon salt

¼ teaspoon black pepper

HELPFUL TIPS

For a nicely browned exterior on the chicken, roll the roulades in 1 tablespoon of melted butter before baking.

1 PREHEAT oven to 400°F. Line a sheet pan with parchment paper.

2 USING a meat mallet, pound the chicken breasts out until about ⅓-inch thick at all parts. Season both sides of each breast with salt, pepper, and paprika.

3 USE your hands to squeeze all excess water from the thawed spinach. Transfer to a mixing bowl.

4 ADD all remaining Stuffing ingredients to the spinach and whisk to combine.

5 SPREAD a large dollop of the Stuffing over top one end of each pounded chicken breast, spreading to cover only the bottom ⅓ of the meat.

6 TIGHTLY roll each chicken breast up, starting on the short end, until chicken is overlapping and you have long roulades. Use toothpicks or tie with baking twine to ensure they keep their shape.

7 BAKE for 22–25 minutes, or until slicing into the largest roulade reveals no pink. Let cool for 5 minutes before serving.

POULTRY

Calories: 370 • Fat: 13.5g • Protein: 57g • Total Carbs: 1g − Fiber: 0g = **Net Carbs: 1g**

GOLDEN GRILLED CHICKEN WITH PEACHES

A SAVORY AND SWEET STONE FRUIT SUPPER

This peachy-keen entrée is a simple, yet stunning dish that is sure to satisfy any palate. The slightly sweet balsamic marinated chicken is delicious all on its own, but it is the addition of grilled fresh peach wedges that makes this recipe a true standout.

SHOPPING LIST

4 boneless, skinless chicken breasts

3 tablespoons balsamic vinegar

2 tablespoons extra virgin olive oil

1 tablespoon sugar substitute

1 teaspoon minced garlic

Vegetable oil, for grill

1 large peach, pitted and cut
　　into thick wedges

HELPFUL TIPS

When grilling the peaches, you want to get them marked by the grill and then off the heat. Grilling them on only one side is best, as that will ensure that they do not overcook and fall apart.

1 PLACE chicken breasts in a food storage container or square baking dish.

2 WHISK together balsamic vinegar, olive oil, sugar substitute, and garlic to create a marinade.

3 POUR marinade over the chicken, cover, and refrigerate for 1 hour, flipping halfway through.

4 GENEROUSLY oil a grill or grill pan and preheat on high heat.

5 REMOVE chicken breasts from marinade. Grill for 8–10 minutes on each side, or until slicing into the thickest part reveals no pink.

6 PLACE the peach wedges on the grill and cook for only 1 minute, just until grill marks have appeared.

7 SERVE each chicken breast topped with 2–3 wedges of grilled peach.

POULTRY

Calories: 320 • Fat: 9g • Protein: 52.5g • Total Carbs: 4.5g – Fiber: 0.5g = **Net Carbs: 4g**

GROUND TURKEY ENCHILADA CASSEROLE

WITH GREEN TOMATOES

Typically made with yellow corn tortillas, my take on the Enchilada Casserole uses thinly sliced, firm, and slightly tart green tomatoes as the starch layer. It's all the flavors you love in an enchilada, without all the carbs!

SHOPPING LIST

Nonstick cooking spray

1 tablespoon olive oil

2 pounds lean ground turkey

2 teaspoons chili powder

2 teaspoons minced garlic

¾ teaspoon salt

½ teaspoon black pepper

¼ teaspoon ground cumin

½ cup diced red onion

½ cup diced red bell pepper

1 (8-ounce) can tomato sauce

½ cup sliced black olives

¼ cup cilantro, chopped

2 green tomatoes, thinly sliced

2 cups shredded Mexican cheese blend, divided

½ cup sour cream

HELPFUL TIPS

A layer of thinly sliced yellow squash can be substituted for the green tomatoes, although you may need to increase the baking time to 40 minutes to ensure the squash is tender.

1 PREHEAT oven to 375°F. Spray a 13x9-inch baking dish with nonstick cooking spray.

2 HEAT olive oil in a large skillet over medium-high heat, until nearly smoking hot.

3 ADD the ground turkey, chili powder, garlic, salt, pepper, and cumin to the skillet. Brown the ground turkey, crumbling it as it cooks.

4 ADD the onion and bell pepper to the skillet and sauté with the ground turkey for 3 minutes, just until onions begin to sweat.

5 STIR tomato sauce, black olives, and cilantro into the skillet. Bring up to a simmer and remove from heat.

6 SPREAD ½ of the turkey mixture across the bottom of the prepared baking dish. Top with the sliced green tomatoes and ½ of the shredded cheese.

7 SPREAD the remaining turkey mixture over the first layer and top with the remaining shredded cheese.

8 BAKE for 30–35 minutes, or until cheese is lightly browned and meat is bubbly hot.

9 LET cool for 5 minutes before serving topped with a dollop of sour cream.

Calories: 355 • Fat: 23g • Protein: 33g • Total Carbs: 6g − Fiber: 2g = **Net Carbs: 4g**

FARMHOUSE CHICKEN

WHOLE CHICKEN ROASTED IN A DUTCH OVEN

When it comes to cooking, it is essential that you have a go-to recipe for roasting a whole chicken. This recipe browns the turkey on the stovetop to crisp the skin before transferring to the oven to cook low and slow for maximum juiciness.

SHOPPING LIST

1 (4–5 pound) whole chicken, giblets discarded

Salt and black pepper

Garlic powder

Paprika

2 tablespoons olive oil

1 yellow onion, cut into wedges

3 stalks celery, cut into 2–inch lengths

2 sprigs rosemary

2 sprigs thyme

HELPFUL TIPS

To substitute the fresh herbs, ¾ teaspoon of dried rosemary and ¾ teaspoon of dried thyme can be used in a pinch.

1 PLACE oven rack in the second-lowest position. Preheat oven to 250°F.

2 PAT chicken dry with paper towels. Season all surfaces of the skin generously with salt, pepper, garlic powder, and paprika.

3 HEAT olive oil in a Dutch oven over medium-high heat.

4 PLACE chicken into the Dutch oven, breast-side down. Cook for 5 minutes, or until skin has lightly browned.

5 CAREFULLY flip chicken. Add the onion and celery to the Dutch oven, surrounding the chicken. Let cook on stove for an additional 5 minutes.

6 TOP the chicken with sprigs of fresh herbs.

7 COVER Dutch oven and transfer to the oven. Bake for 1½ hours, or until a meat thermometer inserted into the thickest part of the breast reads 165°F.

8 LET rest for 10 minutes before carving. Serve with vegetables from the Dutch oven and drizzle with pan juices.

POULTRY

Calories: 365 • Fat: 17g • Protein: 49g • Total Carbs: 1.5g – Fiber: 0g = **Net Carbs: 1.5g**

BARBECUE CHICKEN LEGS

FULL-SIZED DRUMSTICKS IN HOMEMADE BARBECUE SAUCE

A family-favorite, Barbecue Chicken-Legs are the perfect protein that you can pick right up. My homemade barbecue sauce has no added sugars, but a whole lot of added flavor, so there's no reason to reach for a bottle of the corn syrupy store-bought stuff!

SHOPPING LIST

Nonstick cooking spray

2 pounds chicken legs (not drumettes)

BARBECUE SAUCE

1 (8-ounce) can tomato sauce

¼ cup sugar substitute

2 teaspoons white vinegar

1½ teaspoons liquid smoke

1 teaspoon Worcestershire sauce

1 teaspoon minced garlic

½ teaspoon onion powder

¾ teaspoon salt

½ teaspoon black pepper

HELPFUL TIPS

Be sure to purchase ordinary tomato sauce (not pasta sauce) for this recipe. You should also check the label to make sure there is no added sugar or corn syrup.

1 PREHEAT oven to 450°F. Line a sheet pan with aluminum foil and spray foil with nonstick cooking spray.

2 IN a large mixing bowl, whisk together all Barbecue Sauce ingredients.

3 REMOVE ⅓ of the Barbecue Sauce and reserve to baste the chicken later.

4 ADD the chicken legs to the sauce in the mixing bowl and toss to fully coat.

5 TRANSFER the coated legs to the prepared sheet pan.

6 BAKE for 15 minutes.

7 BASTE the legs with the reserved ⅓ of Barbecue Sauce and return to the oven.

8 BAKE for 15–30 additional minutes, or until a meat thermometer inserted into the thickest part registers 175°F. Serve immediately.

POULTRY

Calories: 305 • Fat: 11g • Protein: 44.5g • Total Carbs: 3.5g – Fiber: 1g = **Net Carbs: 2.5g**

MEATS

CONTENTS

PORTABELLA POT ROAST

ITALIAN-STYLE POT ROAST WITH MEATY SLICED MUSHROOMS

With large strips of portabella mushroom, there's no reason to miss the potatoes in this Italian-inspired take on the classic pot roast. Mushrooms are great at absorbing other flavors and they do just that here, while also lending some of their own flavor to the tender chuck roast and its gravy.

SHOPPING LIST

1 tablespoon olive oil

1 boneless beef chuck roast
   (about 3 pounds)

Salt and black pepper

2 teaspoons minced garlic

3 portabella mushroom caps,
   sliced into thick strips

1 red onion, large chopped

2 bay leaves

2½ cups beef broth

½ cup dry red wine

2 tablespoons tomato paste

1 teaspoon Italian seasoning

½ teaspoon salt

½ teaspoon black pepper

1 PREHEAT oven to 325°F.

2 HEAT olive oil in a Dutch oven over high heat, until almost smoking hot.

3 GENEROUSLY season chuck roast with salt and pepper. Place in the hot Dutch oven and brown on both sides, adding the garlic as you brown the second side.

4 REMOVE from heat and top the meat with the mushrooms, red onion, and bay leaves.

5 WHISK together all remaining ingredients and pour over top all in the Dutch oven.

6 COVER and bake for 2 hours, or until meat is fork-tender.

7 SERVE meat and vegetables drizzled with juices from the pan.

HELPFUL TIPS

For a creamier gravy, transfer pan juices to a saucepan and simmer rapidly, until reduced by about ⅓. Remove from heat, and stir in 6 tablespoons of butter.

MEATS

Calories: 380 • Fat: 16g • Protein: 49g • Total Carbs: 4.5g − Fiber: 1g = **Net Carbs: 3.5g**

BALSAMIC MARINATED SKIRT STEAK

GRILLED AND THINLY SLICED FOR MAXIMUM TENDERNESS

Skirt steak is rich in flavor that us chef's prefer, but it can be a difficult cut of meat to prepare...unless you know what you are doing. In this recipe, I ensure foolproof results by marinating the steak in balsamic vinegar to help tenderize it before grilling.

SHOPPING LIST

2 pounds skirt steak

¼ cup balsamic vinegar

3 tablespoons olive oil, plus more for grill

2 tablespoons finely diced red onion

2 teaspoons Worcestershire sauce

2 teaspoons minced garlic

½ teaspoon salt

½ teaspoon black pepper

HELPFUL TIPS

Skirt steak should be served medium-rare at most, as it will get very tough if overcooked.

1 PLACE skirt steak in a food storage container or square baking dish.

2 WHISK together all remaining ingredients to create a marinade.

3 POUR marinade over the skirt steak and flip to coat on both sides.

4 COVER and refrigerate steak for at least 2 hours (and no more than 6), flipping halfway through.

5 OIL a grill or grill pan and preheat on high heat.

6 REMOVE steak from marinade and grill for 5 minutes on each side for medium-rare.

7 LET rest for 10 minutes before thinly slicing against the grain.

MEATS

Calories: 435 • Fat: 23.5g • Protein: 48g • Total Carbs: 1.5g – Fiber: 0g = **Net Carbs: 1.5g**

JAMAICAN JERK BONELESS RIBS

ISLAND SPICED COUNTRY-STYLE RIBS

We're taking a trip to the Caribbean with these tender and meaty ribs rubbed with a Jamaican jerk seasoning. And even though we're on the beach in this Caribbean fantasy, there's no need to toss the bones out into the sand, as these island escapes are boneless and mess-free.

SHOPPING LIST

2 pounds boneless country-style ribs

Juice of 1 lime

1 tablespoon olive oil

2 teaspoons minced garlic

2 green onions, minced

¾ teaspoon ground allspice

1 teaspoon dried thyme

1 teaspoon sugar substitute

½ teaspoon onion powder

½ teaspoon salt

½ teaspoon black pepper

¼ teaspoon cayenne pepper

¼ cup chicken broth or stock

1 PREHEAT oven to 350°F.

2 PLACE ribs in a large mixing bowl. Add all remaining ingredients, except chicken broth, and toss to fully coat. Transfer the seasoned ribs to a baking dish.

3 BAKE for 20 minutes.

4 REDUCE oven temperature to 250°F.

5 FLIP ribs and pour chicken broth into the baking dish. Cover with aluminum foil.

6 BAKE for 2 hours at the reduced temperature, or until meat is fork-tender. Serve immediately.

HELPFUL TIPS

This recipe can also be used to make 2 pounds of pan-seared pork chops. Simply cook in a greased skillet over medium-high heat for 5 minutes on each side, or until the internal temperature of the chops reaches 145°F. With this method, you should omit the chicken stock.

MEATS

Calories: 400 • Fat: 22g • Protein: 45g • Total Carbs: 1.5g – Fiber: 0g = **Net Carbs: 1.5g**

ITALIAN SAUSAGE BOLOGNESE

OVER ZUCCHINI NOODLES

These zucchini noodles are no baloney! By using an ordinary vegetable peeler, they are super easy to prepare, but with extraordinary results. Wide like fettuccine, they make the perfect low-carb bed for the robust Bolognese meat sauce in this recipe.

SHOPPING LIST

2 tablespoons extra virgin olive oil

1 pound ground Italian sausage, without casings

½ cup diced yellow onion

1 stalk celery, diced

2 teaspoons minced garlic

1 (15-ounce can) tomato sauce

¼ cup dry red wine

¼ cup beef stock or broth

2 tablespoons tomato paste

2 tablespoons chopped fresh basil

1 teaspoon Italian seasoning

¾ teaspoon salt

½ teaspoon black pepper

3 zucchini

Grated Parmesan cheese, for topping

HELPFUL TIPS

You can also use a vegetable spiralizer to make even smaller, almost spaghetti-like strands of zucchini. These only need to be dipped in boiling water for around 20 seconds to cook.

1 HEAT olive oil in a large skillet over medium-high heat, until nearly smoking hot. Place a large pot of water over high heat to bring to a boil.

2 ADD the ground sausage to the skillet and brown, crumbling it as it cooks. Drain excess grease.

3 ADD the onion, celery, and garlic to the skillet and sauté with the sausage for 4 minutes, just until onions begin to sweat.

4 STIR tomato sauce, red wine, beef broth, tomato paste, basil, Italian seasoning, salt, and pepper into the skillet.

5 BRING the sauce up to a simmer, reduce heat to low, cover and let simmer 10 minutes.

6 MEANWHILE, use a vegetable peeler to slice the zucchini into long and thin ribbons.

7 ADD the zucchini ribbons to the pot of boiling water and cooker for just 1 minute. Drain and rinse under warm water to bring their temperature down and slow the cooking process.

8 SERVE the Bolognese Sauce over the zucchini noodles. Top with grated Parmesan cheese, if desired.

MEATS

Calories: 470 • Fat: 34g • Protein: 24g • Total Carbs: 13g – Fiber: 4g = **Net Carbs: 9g**

ROASTED RATATOUILLE WITH SAUSAGE

BURSTING WITH A MEDLEY OF COLORFUL VEGETABLES

While traditionally ratatouille is nearly a stew, this recipe bakes it like a casserole. Sliced Italian sausage makes this into a full meal that is not only amazingly colorful, but amazingly flavorful as well. While this is higher in net carbs than many of the other recipes in this book, portion sizes are large and those carbs are coming from fresh, healthy vegetables.

SHOPPING LIST

Nonstick cooking spray

5 Italian sausage links, cooked and sliced

1 medium eggplant, chopped

2 zucchini, chopped

2 yellow squash, chopped

1 red onion, chopped

1 red bell pepper, chopped

1 (8-ounce) can tomato sauce

2 tablespoons extra virgin olive oil

1 tablespoon red wine vinegar

2 teaspoons minced garlic

2 teaspoons Italian seasoning

1 teaspoon salt

¾ teaspoon black pepper

1 PREHEAT oven to 375°F. Spray a 13x9-inch baking dish with nonstick cooking spray.

2 IN a large mixing bowl, toss together all ingredients, coating vegetables with the sauce and spices.

3 TRANSFER the mixed ingredients to the prepared baking dish and spread to evenly disperse.

4 BAKE for 1 hour, or until vegetables are tender and have cooked down considerably. Serve immediately.

HELPFUL TIPS

This is great when topped with grated Parmesan cheese before serving. Or try topping with 2 cups of shredded mozzarella cheese, and placing under the broiler to brown!

MEATS

Calories: 350 • Fat: 26.5g • Protein: 15g • Total Carbs: 13.5g − Fiber: 5.5g = **Net Carbs: 8g**

THE PERFECT RIBEYE STEAK

HOW TO GRILL OR BROIL A RIBEYE STEAK

You can't be a chef without grilling a great steak and you can't grill a great steak without starting with a great cut of meat. The ribeye is protein perfection with a marvelous marbling of fat throughout, and a rich flavor that you don't have to make a reservation at a steakhouse to savor. This recipe breaks down the basics of preparing ribeye steaks at home, either grilled or broiled, and without the steakhouse prices.

SHOPPING LIST

Thick-cut ribeye steaks
    (about 1-inch thick)

Olive oil

Montreal steak seasoning

HELPFUL TIPS

The nutritional information for this recipe is for 1 (8-ounce) ribeye steak with 1 teaspoon of olive oil.

Seasoning: Any blend of spices can be used to season your steaks in place of the Montreal steak seasoning (my favorite). A generous amount of salt, black pepper, garlic powder, and onion powder is a good all-purpose steak seasoning.

1 LET the steaks sit at room temperature for 20 minutes before cooking.

2 DRIZZLE steaks with a teaspoon of olive oil and generously season both sides with Montreal steak seasoning.

3 AFTER cooking according to the specific directions below, let steaks rest under aluminum foil for 10 minutes before serving.

To Grill: Oil and preheat a grill or grill pan to high heat. Place the seasoned steaks on the grill and let cook, without moving, for about 5 minutes on the first side. Flip and cook an additional 4 minutes on the opposite side.

To Broil: Place oven rack about 6 inches below the broiler. Broil for 5 minutes on the first side. Flip and cook for an additional 4 minutes on the opposite side.

Testing for Doneness: Using your finger, poking the steaks should show them to feel firm around the edges, but still have a bit of give in the center. If you have any doubt over this method, use a meat thermometer, removing the steaks from the grill or broiler when the thermometer registers 130°F for medium-rare, 140°F for medium, or 150°F for medium-well.

MEATS

Calories: 565 · Fat: 45g · Protein: 42.5g · Total Carbs: 0g — Fiber: 0g = **Net Carbs: 0g**

HAWAIIAN HAM STEAKS

GRILLED HAM IN A SWEET AND SOUR TERIYAKI SAUCE

Though I haven't figured out a way to make pineapples low-carb, the sweet and sour glaze on these grilled Hawaiian Ham Steaks brings all the flavors you'd expect, without the carbs. You've got plenty of sweetness and a little bit of acid, a perfect complement to the salty ham.

SHOPPING LIST

2 pounds fully-cooked ham steaks

¼ cup teriyaki sauce (see tip)

3 tablespoons sugar substitute

2 tablespoons tomato paste

2 teaspoons white vinegar

Vegetable oil, for grill

HELPFUL TIPS

Look for teriyaki sauce that is thin, like soy sauce. We buy Kikkoman brand with an orange cap. Thicker marinades are typically full of sugar. In a pinch, you can simply use soy sauce.

1 PLACE ham steaks in a food storage container or square baking dish.

2 WHISK together all remaining ingredients, except vegetable oil, to create a marinade.

3 POUR marinade over the hams steaks and toss to coat. Let rest as you preheat the grill.

4 OIL a grill or grill pan and preheat on high heat.

5 FLIP ham steaks to fully coat in marinade and then place on the grill. Grill for 4–5 minutes on each side, just until well-marked and hot throughout.

MEATS

Calories: 360 • Fat: 15g • Protein: 39g • Total Carbs: 3g − Fiber: 0g = **Net Carbs: 3g**

MUSTARD-CRUSTED LONDON BROIL

THINLY SLICED STEAK WITH A WHOLE GRAIN MUSTARD TOPPING

When cooked medium-rare and thinly sliced, London broil can go toe to toe with far more expensive cuts of steak. You can often get a steak large enough to feed the whole family for the cost of just one New York strip... And to be entirely honest, I prefer a well-cooked (but NOT well done) London broil like this to a strip steak!

SHOPPING LIST

2 tablespoons vegetable oil

1 (2½ pound) London broil steak (we use the shoulder cut)

Salt and black pepper

¼ cup prepared whole grain mustard (see tip)

1 tablespoon minced red onion

½ teaspoon minced garlic

HELPFUL TIPS

The whole grain mustard referred to in this recipe should be labeled as either "whole grain" or "coarse" with whole mustard seeds visible within it. Other mustards labeled as Dijon or "deli" may be extremely spicy, which is fine, as long as you can take the heat.

1 PREHEAT oven to 400°F.

2 HEAT vegetable oil in a large skillet over medium-high heat, until almost smoking hot.

3 GENEROUSLY season the steak with salt and pepper.

4 PLACE steak into the hot skillet and brown on each side for 3 minutes. Transfer browned steak to a roasting pan.

5 IN a small mixing bowl, combine mustard, onion, and garlic. Spread over the top of the browned steak.

6 BAKE for 10–15 minutes, or until a meat thermometer inserted into the thickest part reads 135°F for medium-rare.

7 COVER with aluminum foil and let rest for 10 minutes before slicing against the grain.

MEATS

Calories: 330 • Fat: 14g • Protein: 43.5g • Total Carbs: 0.5g – Fiber: 0g = **Net Carbs: 0.5g**

DRY RUBBED BARBECUE SPARERIBS

TENDER PORK RIBS WITH FLAVOR TO SPARE

Ribs don't always need a sticky-sweet sauce to hit the spot. This recipe sticks with only a barbecue dry rub that packs a punch of barbecue flavor, but without a sugary sauce. For even more flavor, I like to grill them after baking, but that choice is yours!

SHOPPING LIST

Nonstick cooking spray

2 large racks pork spareribs
    (3–4 pounds)

Vegetable oil, for grill

DRY RUB

3 tablespoons vegetable oil

2 tablespoons sugar substitute

2 tablespoons paprika

1 tablespoon liquid smoke

2 teaspoons salt

2 teaspoons onion powder

2 teaspoons garlic powder

1 teaspoon black pepper

HELPFUL TIPS

For a great picnic meal, serve alongside my refreshing Superfood Slaw (recipe page: 47).

1 PREHEAT oven to 290°F. Spray a sheet pan with nonstick cooking spray.

2 USING a fork, whisk together all Dry Rub ingredients.

3 USING your fingers, spread the Dry Rub over the entire surface of the ribs, adding more of the rub to the side the meat is on than the opposite side (with the bones).

4 PLACE the rubbed ribs, meat-side up, on the sheet pan. Cover pan tightly with aluminum foil.

5 BAKE for 2 hours, or until ribs easily pull apart. You can serve the ribs as is, or continue onto the grill for even more flavor.

6 OIL and preheat a grill pan to high heat.

7 PLACE baked ribs on the grill and cook for 5 minutes on each side, just to add a nice char.

8 FOR best flavor, serve the finished ribs drizzled with juices from the sheet pan they were roasted on.

MEATS

Calories: 365 • Fat: 32.5g • Protein: 18.5g • Total Carbs: 2g − Fiber: 0.5g = **Net Carbs: 1.5g**

AUTUMN PORK ROAST

CENTER-CUT PORK LOIN THAT IS FULL OF FALL FLAVORS

The leaves are changing, the temperature is dropping, and the sun is hiding behind the clouds… At least, that's what I remember Autumn being like, but I've been living in sunny Florida so long that it's hard to remember. No matter where you live, and what time of year, the spices used in this Autumn Pork Roast are sure to season up your day.

SHOPPING LIST

1 center-cut pork loin roast
  (about 3 pounds)

DRY RUB

1 tablespoon olive oil

1 tablespoon sugar substitute

2 teaspoons cider vinegar

1 teaspoon ground cinnamon

¾ teaspoon salt

½ teaspoon black pepper

½ teaspoon dried thyme

½ teaspoon ground allspice

HELPFUL TIPS

The weights and shapes of pork loin roasts often vary, so it is best to rely on your meat thermometer when checking for doneness.

1 PREHEAT oven to 450°F.

2 PLACE pork roast in a roasting pan.

3 USING a fork, whisk together all Dry Rub ingredients.

4 USING your fingers, spread the Dry Rub over the entire surface of the roast.

5 BAKE for 10 minutes.

6 REDUCE oven temperature to 250°F.

7 CONTINUE baking for 1 additional hour, or until a meat thermometer inserted into the thickest part of the roast registers 145°F.

8 LET rest 10 minutes before slicing.

MEATS

Calories: 345 • Fat: 10.5g • Protein: 59g • Total Carbs: 0.5g – Fiber: 0g = **Net Carbs: 0.5g**

SALISBURY STEAK MARSALA

GROUND SIRLOIN PATTIES WITH A MUSHROOM AND WINE SAUCE

Salisbury Steak isn't just a frozen dinner in a nondescript brown gravy. This recipe uses ground sirloin to make a satisfying Salisbury Steak with a Marsala wine sauce that is more flavorful than the boring old brown gravy.

SHOPPING LIST

STEAK

1½ pounds ground sirloin

1 large egg, beaten

¼ cup grated Parmesan cheese

¼ cup minced red onion

1½ teaspoons Worcestershire sauce

1 teaspoon minced garlic

½ teaspoon onion powder

¾ teaspoon salt

½ teaspoon black pepper

MARSALA

1 tablespoon olive oil

¼ cup diced red onion

8 ounces sliced baby bella mushrooms

¼ cup Marsala wine

½ cup heavy cream

1 teaspoon beef base

1 tablespoon chopped fresh parsley

HELPFUL TIPS

Marsala wine that is labeled "Cream Marsala" is the best for cooking.

1 IN a large mixing bowl, use your hands to combine all Steak ingredients. Form into 4 equal-sized oval patties.

2 HEAT olive oil in a large skillet over medium-high heat.

3 ADD steak patties to the skillet and cook until well browned, about 5 minutes on each side. Transfer to a plate. Drain most of the grease from the skillet.

4 REDUCE heat to medium. Add the onion and mushrooms to the skillet and sauté for 5–7 minutes, until mushrooms are nearly tender.

5 DEGLAZE the skillet with the wine, scraping any browned bits from the bottom of the skillet.

6 STIR the heavy cream and beef base into the skillet.

7 RETURN steak patties to the skillet and flip to coat in the sauce. Bring the sauce up to a simmer. Let simmer for 4 minutes.

8 SEASON sauce with salt and pepper to taste. Sprinkle chopped parsley over steak and sauce before serving.

MEATS

Calories: 460 • Fat: 27g • Protein: 41g • Total Carbs: 6g – Fiber: 1.5g = **Net Carbs: 4.5g**

BARBECUE BEEF

SAUCY SHREDDED BEEF, SLOW COOKED TO PERFECTION

Set your slow cooker to SCRUMPTIOUS, because this pulled beef in a homemade barbecue sauce makes for a delicious entrée with more low-carb serving options than you may think. Try it over my Roasted Garlic Mock Mashed Potatoes (recipe page: 176) or with shredded Cheddar cheese and sliced red onion as a Barbecue Beef Pizza atop my Grain-Free Pizza Crust (recipe page: 61).

SHOPPING LIST

1 tablespoon vegetable oil

1 boneless beef chuck roast
  (about 3 pounds)

Salt and black pepper

¾ cup diced yellow onion

BARBECUE SAUCE

1 (15-ounce) can tomato sauce

½ cup sugar substitute

1 tablespoon white vinegar

1 tablespoon liquid smoke

2 teaspoons Worcestershire sauce

2 teaspoons minced garlic

1 teaspoon onion powder

¾ teaspoon salt

¾ teaspoon black pepper

HELPFUL TIPS

Be sure to purchase ordinary tomato sauce (not pasta sauce) for this recipe. You should also check the label to make sure there is no added sugar or corn syrup.

1 HEAT vegetable oil in a large skillet over high heat, until almost smoking hot.

2 GENEROUSLY season chuck roast with salt and pepper. Place in the hot skillet and brown on both sides. Transfer to a slow cooker.

3 REDUCE heat to medium. Add diced onion to the skillet and sauté for 3 minutes, just until onions are translucent. Place over the browned roast in the slow cooker.

4 IN a large mixing bowl, whisk together all Barbecue Sauce ingredients.

5 POUR Barbecue Sauce into the slow cooker and flip the roast to fully coat.

6 SET the slow cooker to low, cover, and let cook for 8 hours.

7 USING a pair of forks, shred the beef into the sauce before serving.

MEATS

Calories: 370 • Fat: 16g • Protein: 48g • Total Carbs: 7g − Fiber: 1.5g = **Net Carbs: 5.5g**

PORK MILANESE

BREADED PORK CUTLETS WITH PARMESAN CHEESE

This essential recipe for breaded pork chops is a simple everyday meal you may just want to eat…every day. I've substituted a mixture of almond flour and Parmesan cheese in place of high-carb breadcrumbs to achieve the exact same texture, but with arguably more flavor.

SHOPPING LIST

1 pound boneless thin-cut pork cutlets

2 large eggs, beaten

½ cup blanched almond flour

⅓ cup grated Parmesan cheese

Salt and black pepper

Garlic powder

2 tablespoons olive oil

Lemon wedges

HELPFUL TIPS

When you are cooking, it is always best to season each element of a dish, however you only need to lightly season the pork and eggs with salt, as the Parmesan cheese in the breadcrumbs adds additional salt content.

1 LAY out pork cutlets. In a separate dish, beat eggs. In a third dish, combine almond flour and Parmesan cheese.

2 LIGHTLY season the pork chops and egg mixture with salt, pepper, and garlic powder.

3 DIP each seasoned pork cutlet into the beaten eggs, flipping to coat. Immediately dip into the almond flour mixture and press down, coating well on both sides.

4 HEAT olive oil in a large skillet over medium-high heat, until nearly smoking hot.

5 PLACE breaded cutlets into the hot pan and cook until golden brown, about 4 minutes on each side. Slice into the thickest piece to ensure that the pork is cooked throughout.

6 SERVE alongside plenty of lemon wedges to squeeze over the breaded pork.

MEATS

Calories: 345 • Fat: 23.5g • Protein: 28.5g • Total Carbs: 2.5g – Fiber: 1.5g = **Net Carbs: 1g**

BACON-WRAPPED PORK TENDERLOIN

BECAUSE EVEN PORK IS BETTER WITH BACON

While rolling the leanest cut of pork in bacon may seem counter-productive, the fat in the bacon actually helps make this pork tenderloin even more tender. But let's get real for a second… The real reason this pork tenderloin is wrapped in bacon that is roasted to crispy perfection is, well, because it's delicious.

SHOPPING LIST

1 pork tenderloin (about 1¼ pounds)

Salt and black pepper

Garlic powder

1 tablespoon finely chopped fresh sage

6 slices bacon

1 tablespoon olive oil

HELPFUL TIPS

We always look for bacon that is labeled as having no-added-sugar. Those hidden sugar carbs add up!

1 PREHEAT oven to 375°F.

2 GENEROUSLY season pork tenderloin with salt, pepper, garlic powder, and the tablespoon of chopped sage.

3 LAY out the 6 strips of bacon. Place the seasoned tenderloin over top of the bacon and tightly wrap the bacon up and around the meat. Secure with kitchen twine.

4 HEAT olive oil in a large skillet over medium-high heat, until almost smoking hot.

5 PLACE the wrapped tenderloin in the hot skillet and brown on all sides. The bacon should be nearly crisp on the outside. Transfer to a roasting pan.

6 BAKE for 20–25 minutes, or until a meat thermometer inserted into the thickest part registers 145°F.

7 LET rest for 10 minutes before slicing.

MEATS

Calories: 310 • Fat: 20g • Protein: 31g • Total Carbs: 0.5g – Fiber: 0g = **Net Carbs: 0.5g**

MEXICAN LASAGNA

WITH GROUND SIRLOIN AND CREAMY PEPPER-JACK FILLING

This lasagna clearly lost its way and somehow ended up in Tijuana. Thankfully, our faithful lasagna's travels have brought it back with a whole new flavor profile that is different, but just as delicious. Now then, I don't know where along its travels the lasagna lost its noodles, but I swear I think that lasagna is losing weight.

SHOPPING LIST

Nonstick cooking spray

2 tablespoons olive oil

2 pounds ground sirloin

1 green bell pepper, diced

½ cup diced red onion

2 tablespoons chili powder

1 tablespoon ground cumin

2 teaspoons minced garlic

1 teaspoon salt

¾ teaspoon black pepper

½ teaspoon garlic powder

¼ teaspoon cayenne pepper

1 (14.5-ounce) can diced
    tomatoes, with liquid

CHEESE FILLING

15 ounces ricotta cheese

2 cups shredded pepper-Jack cheese

1 large egg

2 tablespoons chopped fresh cilantro

½ teaspoon onion powder

¼ teaspoon salt

TOPPING

2 cups shredded Mexican cheese blend

1 PREHEAT oven to 350°F. Spray a 13x9-inch baking dish with nonstick cooking spray.

2 HEAT olive oil in a large skillet over medium-high heat, until nearly smoking hot.

3 ADD the ground sirloin to the skillet and brown well, crumbling it as it cooks. Drain any excess grease.

4 ADD the bell pepper, onion, chili powder, cumin, garlic, salt, pepper, garlic powder, and cayenne to the skillet and sauté with the sirloin for 4 minutes, just until peppers begin to soften.

5 STIR in diced tomatoes and bring up to a simmer. Reduce heat to low and let simmer 5 minutes, stirring occasionally.

6 IN a large mixing bowl, whisk together all Cheese Filling ingredients.

7 SPREAD all of the ground sirloin mixture across the bottom of the prepared baking dish.

8 TOP the sirloin with the Cheese Filling and smooth it out to fill in any gaps. Top all with the shredded Mexican cheese blend.

9 BAKE for 45–50 minutes, or until cheese is golden brown. Let cool for 10 minutes before serving.

MEATS

Calories: 375 • Fat: 25g • Protein: 30g • Total Carbs: 5.5g − Fiber: 1g = **Net Carbs: 4.5g**

CARAMELIZED ONION MEATLOAF

KETCHUP CAN'T COMPETE WITH MY CARAMELIZED ONION TOPPING

Meatloaf is a comfort food mainstay that can sometimes feel a bit… dated. This recipe cuts the sugary ketchup and brings in a bounty of beautifully-sweet caramelized onions. It's a modern take on a family classic that makes meatloaf a dish worthy of serving company.

SHOPPING LIST

Nonstick cooking spray

MEATLOAF

2 pounds lean ground beef

½ cup shredded Cheddar cheese

½ cup grated Parmesan cheese

¼ cup finely diced yellow onion

2 large eggs, beaten

2 tablespoons tomato paste

2 teaspoons minced garlic

2 teaspoons balsamic vinegar

1½ teaspoons Italian seasoning

¾ teaspoon salt

½ teaspoon onion powder

½ teaspoon black pepper

TOPPING

1 tablespoon olive oil

1 tablespoon unsalted butter

1 large yellow onion, thinly sliced

2 teaspoons balsamic vinegar

1 PREHEAT oven to 350°F. Spray a 9x5-inch loaf pan with nonstick cooking spray.

2 IN a large mixing bowl, use your hands to combine all Meatloaf ingredients.

3 TRANSFER the meatloaf mixture to the prepared baking dish and use your hands to form an even top.

4 BAKE for 45 minutes.

5 MEANWHILE, start the Topping by heating olive oil and butter in a skillet over medium heat.

6 ADD the sliced yellow onion to the skillet and sauté, stirring only occasionally, for 15 minutes. Onions should be nearly caramelized.

7 ADD the balsamic vinegar to the onions and continue sautéing for 5 additional minutes.

8 TOP the partially baked meatloaf with the caramelized onions and return to the oven.

9 BAKE an additional 25–30 minutes, or until a meat thermometer inserted into the center registers 165°F. Let rest 10 minutes before slicing.

HELPFUL TIPS

By using lean ground beef, the meatloaf shrinks far less as it cooks, while the eggs and cheese in the mixture help keep it moist.

MEATS

Calories: 290 • Fat: 17.5g • Protein: 30g • Total Carbs: 3.5g – Fiber: 0.5g = **Net Carbs: 3g**

GRILLED ROSEMARY DIJON PORK CHOPS

CHOP SOME FRESH ROSEMARY FOR THESE SUCCULENT CHOPS

Mustard makes for an instant pork marinade in this essential recipe you'll want to make time and time again. The fresh, forest-y aroma of rosemary helps cut through the strong flavor of the Dijon for a grilled pork chop with perfect balance.

SHOPPING LIST

4 large pork chops, about 1-inch thick

2 tablespoons olive oil, plus more for grill

2 tablespoons Dijon mustard

1 tablespoon chopped fresh rosemary

1 teaspoon sugar substitute

¼ teaspoon dried rosemary

¼ teaspoon garlic powder

⅛ teaspoon salt

⅛ teaspoon black pepper

HELPFUL TIPS

Any type of pork chop can be used for this recipe, whether it is bone-in or a boneless loin chop. That said, thick-cut boneless loin chops tend to be easier to find in most stores.

1 PLACE pork chops in a food storage container or square baking dish.

2 WHISK together all remaining ingredients to create a marinade.

3 SPREAD marinade over the pork and toss to coat on all sides. Let rest for 15 minutes at room temperature as you preheat the grill.

4 OIL a grill or grill pan and preheat on high heat.

5 GRILL pork chops for 5–7 minutes on each side, or until a meat thermometer inserted into the thickest chop registers 145°F.

6 LET rest for 5 minutes before serving.

MEATS

Calories: 315 • Fat: 13.5g • Protein: 45g • Total Carbs: 1g – Fiber: 0g = **Net Carbs: 1g**

BRATWURST WITH SAUER-APPLE-KRAUT

A SAVORY, SWEET, AND SOUR SAUSAGE SAUTÉ

Everybody knows that pork and apples are a perfect team, and that bratwurst and sauerkraut are a home run. This recipe hits a grand slam by combining all three in a simple sauté you'd wish you could get at the ballpark. Bases are loaded and you need dinner? Let this recipe be your pinch hitter. For reference, the count is 8 baseball terms I slid into this description!

SHOPPING LIST

1 tablespoon vegetable oil

5 fresh (raw) bratwurst

1 apple, julienned

½ cup water

1 (16-ounce) bag or jar
    sauerkraut, drained well

1 tablespoon sugar substitute

2 tablespoons unsalted butter

HELPFUL TIPS

Low-carb beer can be used in place of the water in this recipe to add a lot more flavor. This will add less than ½ a gram of net carbs per serving.

1 HEAT vegetable oil in a large skillet over medium-high heat.

2 PLACE bratwurst in the hot skillet and brown on all sides.

3 ADD apple and water to the skillet and bring up to a simmer.

4 REDUCE heat to medium-low, cover, and let simmer for 10 minutes. Add additional water if it fully evaporates.

5 UNCOVER and stir in sauerkraut and sugar substitute, sautéing just until kraut is hot, about 2 minutes.

6 REMOVE from heat and stir in butter before serving.

MEATS

Calories: 350 · Fat: 29.5g · Protein: 14g · Total Carbs: 9g − Fiber: 3.5g = **Net Carbs: 5.5g**

SEAFOOD

CONTENTS

TILAPIA WITH BLISTERED TOMATOES

FISH FILLETS WITH A FRESH ITALIAN TOMATO "SAUCE"

With its mild flavor, low-fat content, and loads of protein, it's easy to see why tilapia is one of the most widely consumed fish in the world. It absorbs and enhances almost any cuisine; and Italian is no exception. A touch of citrus and the light kick of garlic combine with fresh, blistered, grape tomatoes to make a meal that will leave you feeling both full and light on your feet.

SHOPPING LIST

2 tablespoons olive oil

4 tilapia fillets

Salt and black pepper

¾ cup grape tomatoes

¼ cup thinly sliced red onion

Juice of ½ lemon

1 teaspoon minced garlic

¼ teaspoon Italian seasoning

2 tablespoons chopped fresh basil

HELPFUL TIPS

Multicolored grape tomatoes can be used in this dish to make for an even more beautiful presentation.

1 PLACE the olive oil in a large sauté pan over medium-high heat.

2 SEASON the tilapia with salt and pepper. Place fillets into the hot pan and let sear for 3 minutes without moving the fish.

3 FLIP tilapia and let cook for 2 additional minutes, or until fish is flaky. Remove from pan and cover with aluminum foil.

4 ADD tomatoes, red onion, lemon juice, garlic, and Italian seasoning to the pan and sauté for 3–4 minutes, just until tomatoes begin to blister. Season to taste with salt and pepper and stir in fresh basil.

5 SERVE the blistered tomato mixture over top of the cooked tilapia.

SEAFOOD

Calories: 180 • Fat: 9g • Protein: 23g • Total Carbs: 2g − Fiber: 0.5g = **Net Carbs: 1.5g**

GRILLED TERIYAKI TUNA STEAKS

RESTAURANT-STYLE TERIYAKI TUNA, COOKED MEDIUM-RARE

In this recipe, teriyaki and tuna go together like peas and carrots, only lower in carbs. Though you can find an Asian tuna dish on just about every restaurant menu these days, they are typically marinated or glazed with a whole lot of sugar. My low-carb marinade is just as flavorful as any fancy eatery, which means that YOU get to be the restaurateur tonight!

SHOPPING LIST

4 (1-inch-thick) tuna steaks

¼ cup teriyaki sauce (see tip)

1 tablespoon sesame oil

1 tablespoon sugar substitute

2 teaspoons cider vinegar

1 teaspoon minced garlic

½ teaspoon onion powder

¼ teaspoon ground ginger

¼ teaspoon black pepper

Vegetable oil, for grill

1 PLACE tuna steaks in a food storage container or square baking dish.

2 WHISK together all remaining ingredients, except vegetable oil, to create a marinade.

3 POUR marinade over the fish, cover, and refrigerate for 1 hour, flipping halfway through.

4 OIL a grill or grill pan and preheat on high heat.

5 REMOVE tuna steaks from marinade and grill for only 3 minutes on each side. Tuna should be cooked on the outside and nearly raw in the center.

HELPFUL TIPS

Look for teriyaki sauce that is thin, like soy sauce. We buy Kikkoman brand with an orange cap. Thicker marinades are typically full of sugar. In a pinch, you can simply use soy sauce.

SEAFOOD

Calories: 220 • Fat: 5g • Protein: 40g • Total Carbs: 2g – Fiber: 0g = **Net Carbs: 2g**

CASHEW-CRUSTED COD

A FANCY FISH RECIPE THAT IS SO SIMPLE, IT'S NUTTY!

If I told you there was a way to make an already wholesome and flavorful fish even more wholesome and flavorful, you'd probably think I was nuts! Exactly! Cashew nuts! These crunchy, buttery, nutritious tree nuts make for a delicious and golden crust. Like the saying I just made up goes: "Yummy is the cod that wears the cashew crown."

SHOPPING LIST

Nonstick cooking spray

4 cod fillets

1 tablespoon unsalted butter, melted

1 teaspoon lemon juice

¼ teaspoon salt

¼ teaspoon black pepper

1 large egg, beaten

½ cup crushed or finely chopped cashews

1   PREHEAT the oven to 375°F. Line a sheet pan with parchment paper.

2   Toss the cod fillets with the butter, lemon juice, salt, and pepper, coating on all sides.

3   DIP the cod fillets into the beaten egg on one side and then press into the crushed cashews.

4   PLACE each fillet, crusted-side up, on the prepared sheet pan.

5   BAKE for 15 minutes, or until the fish easily flakes with a fork. Serve immediately.

HELPFUL TIPS

Any cashews that are leftover after crusting the fish can be sprinkled over top of the fillets before baking to make a thicker or more even crust.

SEAFOOD

Calories: 230 • Fat: 12.5g • Protein: 24g • Total Carbs: 5.5g – Fiber: 0.5g = **Net Carbs: 5g**

SHRIMP AND GRITS

A SOUTHERN CLASSIC, WITHOUT THOSE CLASSIC CARBS

Though everyone in the South has their own take on Shrimp and Grits, I guarantee that nobody has ever had a low-carb take on it.... Well, until now, that is! In this recipe, my entirely grain-free grits are located just to the south of a heaping helping of tender shrimp in a deep and delicious tomato sauce.

SHOPPING LIST

GRITS

1½ cups blanched almond flour

1½ cups water

2 tablespoons unsalted butter

¼ teaspoon salt

¼ teaspoon black pepper

2 ounces cream cheese

SHRIMP

1 tablespoon olive oil

1½ pounds large shrimp, peeled and deveined

⅓ cup diced green bell pepper

Juice of ½ lemon

2 teaspoons minced garlic

1 teaspoon paprika

1 (14.5-ounce) can diced tomatoes, drained

1 tablespoon tomato paste

1 tablespoon chopped fresh parsley

¾ teaspoon dried oregano

¼ teaspoon salt

¼ teaspoon black pepper

1 ADD all Grits ingredients, except cream cheese, to a saucepan over medium-high heat and whisk to combine.

2 STIRRING constantly, bring the grits up to a simmer and cook for 5–6 minutes, until mixture begins to thicken.

3 REMOVE from heat and stir in cream cheese. Let cool for 5 minutes.

4 MEANWHILE, heat oil in a large sauté pan over medium-high heat.

5 ADD the shrimp, bell pepper, lemon juice, garlic, and paprika to the hot pan and toss to evenly coat shrimp with spices.

6 SAUTÉ for 2 minutes before stirring in all remaining Shrimp ingredients.

7 SAUTÉ for an additional 2–4 minutes, just until shrimp are opaque. Serve immediately, spooning the shrimp mixture directly over the grits.

HELPFUL TIPS

For a bit of heat, add a pinch of crushed red pepper flakes to the shrimp as you sauté them.

SEAFOOD

Calories: 350 • Fat: 24g • Protein: 26.5g • Total Carbs: 9.5g − Fiber: 4g = **Net Carbs: 5.5g**

LEMON CAPER COD

SEARED COD IN A PICCATA-STYLE BUTTER SAUCE

Though traditionally served with veal in Italy, cod is the perfect protein to soak up all the bright, buttery flavor of a classic piccata sauce. If you don't believe me, take a bite. It'll taste so good, I guarantee you'll use my new favorite pun: "Piccata-be kidding me!"

SHOPPING LIST

1 tablespoon olive oil

4 cod fillets

Salt and black pepper

Garlic powder

Juice of 1 lemon

2 tablespoons capers, drained

2 tablespoons unsalted butter

1 tablespoon chopped fresh parsley

¼ teaspoon lemon zest

HELPFUL TIPS

Any lean white fish (such as tilapia, grouper, and haddock) can be used in place of the cod in this recipe.

1 PLACE the olive oil in a large sauté pan over medium-high heat.

2 LIGHTLY season the cod with salt, pepper, and garlic powder. Place fillets into the hot pan and let sear for 3 minutes without moving the fish.

3 FLIP cod and let cook for 2 additional minutes, or until fish is flaky.

4 SQUEEZE the lemon juice into the pan.

5 REMOVE from heat and add the capers, butter, parsley, and lemon zest to the pan. Shake the pan until the butter melts into a sauce.

6 SERVE cod fillets drizzled with the sauce from the pan.

SEAFOOD

Calories: 170 • Fat: 10g • Protein: 20g • Total Carbs: 0.5g − Fiber: 0g = **Net Carbs: 0.5g**

GRILLED SALMON WITH RED PEPPER RELISH

A REFRESHINGLY NEW WAY TO TOP GRILLED FISH

Rachel and I eat salmon once a week, so we are always looking for new ways to prepare and serve it. We reeled in a real winner with the Red Pepper Relish in this recipe. It makes a refreshing topping for grilled salmon, adding just enough flavor and acid, without overwhelming the flavor of the fish.

SHOPPING LIST

RED PEPPER RELISH

½ cup diced roasted red peppers, drained

2 tablespoons minced red onion

1 tablespoon extra virgin olive oil

1 tablespoon chopped fresh parsley

2 teaspoons red wine vinegar

1 teaspoon minced garlic

⅛ teaspoon salt

⅛ teaspoon black pepper

SALMON

Vegetable oil, for grill

2 pounds skinless salmon fillets

Juice of ½ lemon

Salt and black pepper

1 COMBINE all Red Pepper Relish ingredients and let marinate at room temperature as you prepare the salmon.

2 OIL a grill or grill pan and preheat on medium-high heat.

3 DRIZZLE salmon with lemon juice and season generously with salt and pepper.

4 GRILL salmon for 4 minutes on each side, or until it easily flakes with a fork.

5 SERVE salmon topped with the Red Pepper Relish.

HELPFUL TIPS

Jarred roasted red peppers are the quickest and easiest way to make this recipe. You can even purchase diced pimentos (which are basically the same as roasted red peppers) to make for even easier prep.

SEAFOOD

Calories: 340 • Fat: 17.5g • Protein: 44.5g • Total Carbs: 2.5g − Fiber: 0g = **Net Carbs: 2.5g**

SPANISH SCALLOP SAUTÉ

WITH TWO TYPES OF OLIVES AND FRESH AVOCADO

The brine of both green and black olives perfectly offsets the natural sweetness of sea scallops in this taste of Spain. It's as if you found a sunken ship just off Costa Blanca… and in that ship you found a treasure chest…and in that chest you found…this recipe!

SHOPPING LIST

1 tablespoon olive oil

1¼ pounds sea scallops, patted dry

Salt and black pepper

½ cup thinly sliced yellow onion

½ cup thinly sliced yellow bell pepper

2 teaspoons minced garlic

1 tomato, diced

¼ cup sliced green olives

¼ cup finely chopped black olives

Juice of ½ lemon

2 tablespoons chopped fresh parsley

1 Hass avocado, pitted, peeled, and chopped

HELPFUL TIPS

Be sure to only season the vegetable mixture with salt to taste after it has cooked, as a lot of the salt in the olives will cook into the dish.

1 HEAT oil in a large skillet over high heat, until nearly smoking hot.

2 LIGHTLY season the scallops with salt and pepper. Add to the hot skillet.

3 LET scallops sear on one side for 2 minutes. Flip and cook for an additional 1½ minutes on the opposite side. Remove scallops and set aside.

4 REDUCE heat to medium. Add the onion to the skillet and sauté for 3 minutes.

5 ADD all remaining ingredients, except avocado, to the skillet and sauté for 5 minutes, or until bell pepper is crisp-tender. Season vegetable mixture with salt and pepper to taste.

6 PLACE the scallops back into the skillet and toss with the hot vegetables to warm back up.

7 TOP with the chopped avocado and serve immediately.

SEAFOOD

Calories: 260 • Fat: 12.5g • Protein: 26g • Total Carbs: 10.5g – Fiber: 2.5g = **Net Carbs: 8g**

FIERY SHRIMP

A FIVE-ALARM FIRE FROM THE OCEAN FLOOR

Sound the shrimp alarm, as things are about to get spicy! With both chili powder and hot pepper sauce, these little guys bring the heat. Thankfully, tomato paste and butter are stirred into the sauce to both balance out the flavors and extinguish the fire.

SHOPPING LIST

1 tablespoon vegetable oil

1½ pounds large shrimp, peeled and deveined

Juice of ½ lemon

1 teaspoon minced garlic

½ teaspoon chili powder

¼ teaspoon salt

¼ teaspoon black pepper

2 tablespoons tomato paste

2 teaspoons hot pepper sauce (such as Tabasco)

3 tablespoons unsalted butter

1 HEAT oil in a large sauté pan over medium-high heat.

2 ADD the shrimp, lemon juice, garlic, chili powder, salt, and pepper to the hot pan and toss to evenly coat shrimp with spices.

3 SAUTÉ for 4 minutes, just until shrimp are opaque.

4 ADD the tomato paste and hot pepper sauce to the skillet and toss to coat shrimp. Cook for an additional 30 seconds, stirring frequently.

5 REMOVE from heat and stir in butter before serving.

HELPFUL TIPS

For a pop of color, serve topped with sliced green onion or chopped fresh parsley. For a burst of freshness, top with fresh lemon zest.

SEAFOOD

Calories: 250 • Fat: 13g • Protein: 30g • Total Carbs: 2.5g − Fiber: 0g = **Net Carbs: 2.5g**

HALIBUT WITH DIJON AND TARRAGON

PAN-SEARED HALIBUT IN A CREAMY MUSTARD SAUCE

Halibut is known as a "flatfish," which is a very fancy fisherman term for fish that are…well, flat. (Think flounder.) But halibut isn't just any flatfish, it is known as the "king of the flatfish," as it can grow up to 700 pounds.

SHOPPING LIST

1 tablespoon olive oil

4 halibut fillets

Salt and black pepper

¼ cup dry white wine (see tip)

2 tablespoons Dijon mustard

1 tablespoon chopped fresh tarragon

¼ teaspoon onion powder

2 tablespoons unsalted butter

HELPFUL TIPS

Substitute ¼ cup of chicken stock and the juice of ½ lemon in place of the wine, if desired.

1 PLACE the olive oil in a large skillet over medium-high heat.

2 LIGHTLY season the halibut with salt and pepper.

3 PLACE seasoned fillets into the hot pan and let sear for 4 minutes without moving the fish.

4 FLIP and let cook for 3 additional minutes, or until fish is flaky and opaque throughout. Remove from skillet and cover with aluminum foil.

5 ADD the white wine, Dijon mustard, tarragon, and onion powder to the skillet and stir to combine. Bring up to a simmer and let cook for 2 minutes.

6 REMOVE from heat and stir in butter to thicken the sauce before drizzling over the cooked halibut.

SEAFOOD

Calories: 320 • Fat: 13.5g • Protein: 47g • Total Carbs: 1g − Fiber: 0g = **Net Carbs: 1g**

ZESTY SALMON

WITH ROASTED FENNEL AND ORANGE ZEST

Fennel is clearly related to dill and you can see it in its fronds. It is also related to carrots, but that relation makes a whole lot less sense. What DOES make sense is pairing the strong, almost anise-like flavor of fennel with the brightness of orange zest in this simple, yet elegant recipe for roasted salmon.

SHOPPING LIST

Nonstick cooking spray

1 bulb fennel

2 pounds skinless salmon fillets

2 tablespoons olive oil

1 tablespoon orange zest

2 teaspoons lemon juice

¼ teaspoon salt

¼ teaspoon black pepper

HELPFUL TIPS

If you are not a fan of fennel, this can also be made without the roasted fennel. Simply place a sprig of rosemary atop each salmon fillet to replace the chopped fennel fronds.

1 PREHEAT oven to 425°F. Generously spray a sheet pan with nonstick cooking spray.

2 REMOVE fennel fronds and reserve. Core fennel bulb and then thinly slice. Arrange the sliced fennel bulb on the prepared sheet pan in a single layer.

3 TOP the sliced fennel bulb with the salmon fillets.

4 FINELY chop fennel fronds and transfer 3 tablespoons to a small mixing bowl. Save or discard remaining fronds.

5 ADD all remaining ingredients to the mixing bowl and whisk to combine. Drizzle over the salmon and fennel bulb.

6 BAKE for 10–13 minutes, just until salmon is easily flaked with a fork.

7 COVER with aluminum foil and let rest for 5 minutes before serving.

SEAFOOD

Calories: 380 • Fat: 21g • Protein: 45g • Total Carbs: 5g – Fiber: 2g = **Net Carbs: 3g**

SHRIMP AND SCALLOP SKEWERS

WITH CILANTRO AND LIME

Isn't everything better in pairs? These Shrimp and Scallop Skewers not only pair two delicate and naturally sweet types of seafood, they also pair the classic flavors of cilantro and lime. They're so good, you're going to want a skewer for each hand— but don't do that unless you've got great coordination—those skewers are sharp!

SHOPPING LIST

Bamboo skewers

12 extra large shrimp, peeled and deveined

12 sea scallops

¼ cup chopped cilantro

3 tablespoons olive oil

1 tablespoon diced red onion

Juice of 1 lime

1 teaspoon lime zest

¼ teaspoon salt

¼ teaspoon black pepper

HELPFUL TIPS

For even more flavor, serve the grilled skewers topped with pats of butter and a squeeze of fresh lime juice.

1 SOAK bamboo skewers in water for at least 30 minutes before preparing.

2 PLACE shrimp and scallops in a large mixing bowl.

3 ADD cilantro and all remaining ingredients to a food processor and pulse until a smooth, but thick marinade.

4 POUR the marinade over the shrimp and scallops and toss to coat. Cover and refrigerate 30 minutes.

5 THREAD a marinated scallop onto a soaked skewer, then a marinated shrimp. Add a second scallop and then a second shrimp to make 4 pieces of seafood on the skewer. Repeat until you've made 6 skewers.

6 PREHEAT a grill or grill pan over high heat.

7 PLACE the skewers on the grill horizontally (so that they do not get stuck between the grates).

8 GRILL for just 2 minutes on each side. Serve immediately.

SEAFOOD

Calories: 180 • Fat: 8.5g • Protein: 22.5g • Total Carbs: 2.5g – Fiber: 0g = **Net Carbs: 2.5g**

MEDITERRANEAN MUSSELS

WITH KALAMATA OLIVES, OREGANO, AND FRESH TOMATOES

I always find that there is something rewarding about food you have to work for. The effort seems to make it taste that much better. The process of cleaning, and then cooking these succulent little jewels of the sea feels like an accomplishment on its own. But there's nothing wrong with deriving all of this dish's pleasure from just eating it; and trust me, once you pop these mussels out of the shell and into your mouth, it will be all the reward you need.

SHOPPING LIST

3 pounds mussels

2 tablespoons olive oil

¼ cup diced red onion

2 cloves garlic, crushed

¼ cup dry white wine

2 plum tomatoes, chopped

¼ cup chopped Kalamata olives

2 tablespoons chopped fresh oregano

½ teaspoon lemon zest

¼ teaspoon dried oregano

¼ teaspoon black pepper

Salt

HELPFUL TIPS

It is always a good idea to check for dead mussels before cooking. Find any shells that are partially open and lightly tap on them several times. If they do not close back up, then they should be discarded.

1 SCRUB and debeard the mussels by pulling the beard downwards, toward the hinged end of the shell. Pull firmly until the beard dislodges.

2 PLACE olive oil in a deep skillet over medium-high heat.

3 ADD the onion and garlic to skillet and sauté for 3 minutes, just until garlic is fragrant.

4 ADD all remaining ingredients, except the cleaned mussels, and bring up to a simmer.

5 ADD the cleaned mussels to the skillet, reduce heat to medium, and cover.

6 COOK for 8–10 minutes, occasionally shaking the pan from side to side to keep the mussels moving. Mussels are done when the shells have opened.

7 SERVE mussels in a shallow bowl, topped with the liquid and vegetables from the skillet.

SEAFOOD

Calories: 250 • Fat: 12g • Protein: 21g • Total Carbs: 11g − Fiber: 2g = **Net Carbs: 9g**

SIDE DISHES

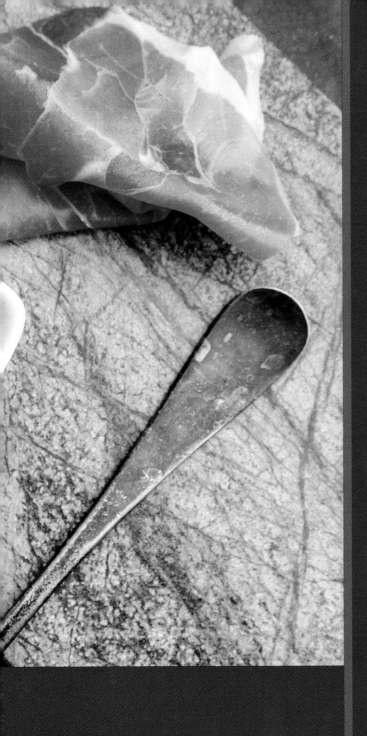

CONTENTS

BREAD AND BUTTER ZUCCHINI PICKLES

SWEET AND SAVORY SQUASH PICKLES

Apparently, this classic sweet and sour brine got its name from Omar and Cora Fanning, a pair of Illinois farmers in the 1920's. They would pickle their undersized cucumbers and barter them with local grocers for common kitchen staples…like bread and butter. Here I've used crisp zucchini to craft a low-carb, sweet and sour salute to those two opportunistic farmers.

SHOPPING LIST

1 pound zucchini, sliced into ⅛-inch discs

3 tablespoons kosher salt

1½ cups cider vinegar

¾ cup sugar substitute

¼ cup minced yellow onion

1 tablespoon mustard seeds

¾ teaspoon celery seeds

½ teaspoon minced garlic

½ teaspoon ground turmeric

⅛ teaspoon ground cloves

4 whole cloves, or an additional ⅛ teaspoon ground cloves

HELPFUL TIPS

When adding salt to the brine, it is best to add a pinch more than what suits your tastes, as the salt will help deliver the flavors of the brine into the zucchini, which can also use that extra salt.

1 PLACE the sliced zucchini in a large bowl and toss with the kosher salt. Cover with ice water and refrigerate for 1 hour to slightly soften the zucchini.

2 DRAIN the softened zucchini well. Rinse and drain again.

3 ADD the remaining ingredients to a saucepot over medium-high heat and whisk to combine. Bring up to a simmer.

4 ADD the drained zucchini to the pot and bring back up to a simmer. Remove from heat and season the brine to taste with additional kosher salt (see tip).

5 LET cool for 15 minutes before transferring the pickles and brine to a large jar or food storage container.

6 CHILL overnight before serving. Store refrigerated for up to 1 month.

SIDES

Calories: 25 • Fat: 0g • Protein: 1g • Total Carbs: 3.5g – Fiber: 1g = **Net Carbs: 2.5g**

SOUTHERN GREEN BEANS

GREEN BEANS WITH BACON, COOKED LOW AND SLOW

If you ask me, there's really only two ways to cook a vegetable: at high heat for a short period, or "low and slow." The high heat method retains the flavors and caramelizes new flavors, while the low and slow method in these Southern Green Beans develops flavors. You take the vegetable past the point of no return, into a tasty and tender territory you never knew existed. Then you plant a fork in that territory, the same way you'd plant a flag. It lets everyone know that you let the green beans cook an entire hour, and that they tasted better for it.

SHOPPING LIST

4 strips bacon, chopped

¼ cup diced onion

1½ pounds green beans, ends snapped

3 cups chicken broth

½ teaspoon onion powder

¼ teaspoon garlic powder

¼ teaspoon black pepper

Salt

HELPFUL TIPS

For the true look of Southern green beans, cut the trimmed beans into 2-inch lengths before cooking.

1   ADD bacon to a medium pot over medium-high heat.

2   SAUTÉ bacon until nearly crisp. Add onion and continue sautéing until bacon is crisp and onion is translucent.

3   ADD all remaining ingredients to the pot and stir.

4   BRING up to a boil. Reduce heat to low and cover.

5   LET simmer for 1 hour, stirring every 20 minutes. Beans should be extremely tender.

6   SEASON with salt to taste before serving.

SIDES

Calories: 145 • Fat: 9.5g • Protein: 6g • Total Carbs: 10.5g − Fiber: 5g = **Net Carbs: 5.5g**

ROASTED BROCCOLI OR BROCCOLINI

THE MOST FLAVORFUL WAY TO PREPARE BROCCOLI

In my last recipe, I praised the virtues of cooking vegetables "low and slow," but this recipe takes the opposite approach. By roasting broccoli at an extremely high temperature, you can actually caramelize it and bring out nutty flavors that you never even knew it could have. Broccolini, or "sweet baby broccoli" as it is sometimes marketed as, is slightly sweeter than ordinary broccoli and can also be prepared in this same method.

SHOPPING LIST

1½ pounds broccoli or broccolini

2 tablespoons olive oil

½ teaspoon red wine vinegar

¼ teaspoon garlic powder

¼ teaspoon salt

¼ teaspoon black pepper

HELPFUL TIPS

This method also works great with cauliflower. Omit the red wine vinegar and add ½ teaspoon of curry powder to make delicious Roasted Curry Cauliflower.

1 PREHEAT oven to 450°F.

2 IN a large mixing bowl, toss broccoli with all remaining ingredients, evenly coating with the olive oil and spices.

3 ARRANGE the coated broccoli on a sheet pan in a single layer.

4 BAKE for 17–20 minutes, until the edges of the broccoli have browned and stems are crisp-tender. Serve immediately.

SIDES

Calories: 115 • Fat: 7.5g • Protein: 5g • Total Carbs: 11g − Fiber: 4.5g = **Net Carbs: 6.5g**

SPAGHETTI SQUASH CARBONARA

TRADITIONAL CARBONARA, WITHOUT THE CARBS

Carbonara is a traditional Italian method for preparing pasta in a creamy sauce made from only egg and aged cheese (either Pecorino or Parmesan). In this recipe, I've kept things almost entirely as they should be, except for one low-carb twist: the substitution of spaghetti squash in place of high-carb spaghetti.

SHOPPING LIST

1 (2- to 3- pound) spaghetti squash

½ cup diced pancetta (may use bacon)

2 large eggs

⅔ cup grated Parmesan cheese

1 tablespoon chopped fresh parsley

¼ teaspoon black pepper

Salt

HELPFUL TIPS

You can also microwave the spaghetti squash by placing the halves, cut side down, in a microwave-safe dish filled with 1 inch of water. Set to high and cook for 6–8 minutes, or until fork-tender.

1 CUT spaghetti squash in half lengthwise. Scrape out seeds and fibrous pulp and discard.

2 USING the tip of a knife, pierce the rind of both halves of the squash in several places to vent while it cooks.

3 PLACE squash halves in a large pot and cover with water. Bring to a boil. Let cook for 20 minutes, or until the rind of the squash is easily pierced with a fork.

4 DRAIN squash and let cool for 5 minutes. Using a fork, scrape the strands of squash out of the rind, separating them as you go. Set aside.

5 PLACE the pancetta in a large skillet over medium heat and cook until crispy, about 5 minutes. Do not drain grease.

6 MEANWHILE, whisk together the eggs, Parmesan cheese, parsley, and pepper. Set aside.

7 ADD the cooked strands of spaghetti squash to the pancetta and grease in the pan. Sauté for just 1 minute to heat the squash.

8 REMOVE pan from heat. While constantly stirring, add the egg mixture to the squash, letting the residual heat in the pan technically cook the eggs without scrambling them. Season with salt to taste and serve immediately.

SIDES

Calories: 215 • Fat: 15.5g • Protein: 14g • Total Carbs: 7g – Fiber: 1.5g = **Net Carbs: 5.5g**

ROASTED GARLIC MOCK MASHED POTATOES

SMASHED CAULIFLOWER WITH CREAMY AND SWEET GARLIC

Garlic gets a bad rap! Sure, it can be strong, and even spicy when eaten raw… but give garlic a good roast, and you've got a whole new flavor—one that is nutty, sweet, and far more subtle. Roasting garlic doesn't just change the flavor, it gives it a velvety smooth texture that makes it the perfect mix-in for these Mock Mashed Potatoes made from smashed cauliflower.

SHOPPING LIST

Cloves of 1 head garlic, peeled

2 tablespoons olive oil

1 medium head cauliflower

¼ cup grated Parmesan cheese

3 tablespoons heavy cream

¼ teaspoon black pepper

Salt

HELPFUL TIPS

If the cauliflower cools down too much before serving, simply microwave for 1–2 minutes to bring it back up to temperature.

1 PREHEAT the oven to 375°F. Fold the edges of a sheet of aluminum foil up to make a bowl.

2 PLACE garlic cloves in the foil bowl and add the olive oil, tossing to coat. Fold aluminum foil over to cover the garlic, creating a packet.

3 BAKE for 40 minutes, or until garlic is fragrant and easily pierced with a fork.

4 BRING a large pot of water to a boil over high heat.

5 CUT cauliflower into small pieces, stem and all. Add to the boiling water and cook for 6 minutes, or until tender.

6 DRAIN cauliflower well, but do not cool. Use a heavy bowl to press the cauliflower down into a colander to drain as much water as possible.

7 ADD the roasted garlic with the oil it was cooked in, drained cauliflower, Parmesan cheese, heavy cream, and pepper to a food processor. Pulse until completely smooth.

8 SEASON with salt to taste before serving.

SIDES

Calories: 160 • Fat: 13.5g • Protein: 5.5g • Total Carbs: 7.5g – Fiber: 2.5g = **Net Carbs: 5g**

SAUTÉED STEAK TOPPERS

SEASONED ONIONS, PEPPERS, AND MUSHROOMS

So you've got a steak and you know how to grill it. Or broil it. Or pan-fry it. But do you know how to top it? Steak sauce can move on over because there's far more flavorful toppers in town. This simple sauté of onions, peppers, mushrooms, and garlic raises the stakes, and I bet you're going to love it more than my puns.

SHOPPING LIST

1 tablespoon vegetable oil

1 tablespoon unsalted butter

1 small red onion, thinly sliced

1 red bell pepper, thinly sliced

8 ounces sliced baby bella mushrooms

1½ teaspoons minced garlic

1 teaspoon balsamic vinegar

1 teaspoon Montreal steak seasoning

HELPFUL TIPS

Montreal steak seasoning is a wonderful, all-purpose, seasoning to keep in your spice cabinet. That said, you can substitute ¼ teaspoon each of salt and black pepper if you are in a pinch.

1 HEAT oil and butter in a large skillet over medium heat, until butter has melted.

2 ADD the onion to the hot skillet and toss to coat with oil and butter.

3 SAUTÉ, stirring only occasionally, until onions have cooked down, about 7 minutes.

4 ADD the bell pepper, mushrooms, and garlic to the skillet. Sauté for an additional 7 minutes, or until mushrooms are tender.

5 ADD the vinegar and Montreal steak seasoning to the skillet. Sauté for 1 additional minute before serving.

SIDES

Calories: 85 • Fat: 6.5g • Protein: 2g • Total Carbs: 6.5g – Fiber: 2g = **Net Carbs: 4.5g**

BARBECUE SWEET POTATO CHIPS

A BETTER CHIP, BAKED UP QUICK

We're all human beings, and part of what makes us so, is our susceptibility to random snack attacks. One fun way to combat them is to plan ahead, and snack smarter, with a batch of these incredible, crispy baked chips. Packed with powerful antioxidants and rich in beta-carotene, these salty-sweet crisps are a snack you can feel good about.

SHOPPING LIST

2 large sweet potatoes, scrubbed

½ teaspoon salt

1½ tablespoons olive oil

SEASONING

1 tablespoon smoked paprika

2 teaspoons sugar substitute

½ teaspoon onion powder

½ teaspoon salt

¼ teaspoon black pepper

HELPFUL TIPS

These will soften if not eaten immediately, however you can bake leftovers in a 450°F oven for 2–3 minutes to crisp them back up.

1 PREHEAT oven to 450°F.

2 USING a mandolin slicer or slicing attachment of a food processor, thinly and evenly slice the sweet potatoes, no more than ⅛ inch thick.

3 TRANSFER the sliced sweet potatoes to a large bowl of water. Stir in ½ teaspoon of salt. Let sit for 10 minutes.

4 DRAIN the sliced sweet potatoes well. Pat dry with paper towels.

5 TOSS the sliced sweet potatoes in the olive oil before spreading in a single layer across 2 sheet pans.

6 BAKE for 7 minutes.

7 COMBINE all Seasoning ingredients and sprinkle over the baked potato chips.

8 RETURN to the oven and bake an additional 5 minutes, just until chips are beginning to brown around the edges. Serve immediately.

SIDES

Calories: 65 · Fat: 3.5g · Protein: 1g · Total Carbs: 8g – Fiber: 1.5g = **Net Carbs: 6.5g**

TENDER ARTICHOKES WITH GARLIC AÏOLI

WHOLE ARTICHOKES THAT YOU EAT BY THE LEAF

Sometimes nature does most of the work for you. In the case of the beautiful, whole artichoke, you may have to remind yourself to stop staring and actually eat the thing. I've had many a great conversation with family and friends with nothing but an artichoke between us. No need to dirty any silverware, it is perfectly polite to pluck the leaves off with your fingers. In fact, it's tradition!

SHOPPING LIST

2 artichokes

1 lemon, quartered

GARLIC AÏOLI

¼ cup mayonnaise

1 clove garlic, smashed

½ teaspoon Dijon mustard

¼ teaspoon lemon juice

⅛ teaspoon salt

⅛ teaspoon black pepper

HELPFUL TIPS

For a nicer presentation (but entirely optional), use kitchen shears to trim the pointed tip of each leaf before cooking.

1 BRING a large pot of water to a boil.

2 USE a chef's knife to trim the top inch from the artichoke in one simple cut (these topmost leaves have no meat on them). Cut stems from the bottom of the artichokes. Discard top leaves and stems.

3 PLACE the trimmed artichokes and lemon in the boiling water.

4 LET boil for 45 minutes, or until the bottom leaves can easily pull away from the rest of the artichoke. Transfer to serving dishes.

5 IN a small mixing bowl, whisk together all Garlic Aïoli ingredients.

6 EAT the artichoke by pulling the leaves off, one at a time. Dip in the Garlic Aïoli and then use your teeth to scrape the meat off of the leaves, then discard each leaf. When you get to the center of the artichoke, scrape off the threads with a spoon to get to the tender artichoke heart.

SIDES

Calories: 245 • Fat: 20.5g • Protein: 3.5g • Total Carbs: 14g − Fiber: 10g = **Net Carbs: 4g**

LOWER-CARB SWEET POTATO MASH

MY MOCK MASH MEETS REAL SWEET POTATO MASH

I've been making Mock Mashed Potatoes out of cauliflower for over a decade now, but I've never made a mash-up like this before! By making this mash from both real sweet potatoes and cauliflower, I've been able to cut the carbs in half without sacrificing flavor or texture. It truly is the best of both worlds.

SHOPPING LIST

2 sweet potatoes, peeled and cut into 2-inch pieces

3 tablespoons unsalted butter

1 (16-ounce) bag frozen cauliflower florets

¼ cup half-and-half

3 tablespoons sugar substitute

¼ teaspoon maple extract

¼ teaspoon ground cinnamon

¼ teaspoon salt

⅛ teaspoon ground nutmeg

HELPFUL TIPS

If the finished dish cools down too much before serving, simply microwave for 1–2 minutes to bring it back up to temperature.

1 BRING a large pot of water to a boil over high heat.

2 ADD sweet potatoes to the boiling water and cook for 15 minutes, or until tender. Drain well, then return to the pot.

3 ADD the butter to the sweet potatoes and use a potato masher to fully mash.

4 MICROWAVE cauliflower florets according to the package directions. Drain any excess water.

5 ADD the drained cauliflower and all remaining ingredients to a food processor. Pulse until completely smooth.

6 FOLD the puréed cauliflower mixture into the mashed sweet potatoes, until all is combined.

7 SEASON to taste with any additional salt and ground cinnamon before serving.

SIDES

Calories: 120 • Fat: 7g • Protein: 2.5g • Total Carbs: 13.5g − Fiber: 3g = **Net Carbs: 10.5g**

PARMESAN EGGPLANT

ROASTED EGGPLANT WITH PARMESAN CHEESE

No, the title of this recipe is not a typo. This is "Parmesan Eggplant" not "Eggplant Parmesan." While these tender cubes of roasted eggplant share a lot of the same flavors as that more famous recipe (minus the tomato sauce), this makes a perfect side dish, rather than an entrée. We all love Eggplant Parmesan for dinner. Now we can have Parmesan Eggplant alongside ANY dinner.

SHOPPING LIST

1 eggplant (about 2 pounds)

2 tablespoons olive oil

1 teaspoon minced garlic

½ teaspoon Italian seasoning

¼ teaspoon black pepper

⅛ teaspoon salt

3 tablespoons grated Parmesan cheese

HELPFUL TIPS

You can add roasted tomatoes to this recipe (to make it more like the flavors of traditional Eggplant Parmesan) by adding 1 cup of grape tomatoes to the pan after the first 10 minutes of baking. This will add less than 2g of net carbs per serving.

1 PREHEAT oven to 425°F.

2 SLICE ends from eggplant and discard. Cut eggplant into 1-inch cubes.

3 IN a large mixing bowl, toss cubed eggplant with olive oil, minced garlic, Italian seasoning, pepper, and salt, evenly coating with the olive oil and spices.

4 ARRANGE the coated eggplant on a sheet pan in a single layer.

5 BAKE for 10 minutes. Toss eggplant and return to the oven.

6 BAKE for an additional 10–15 minutes, just until eggplant is fork tender and golden brown.

7 Toss the roasted eggplant in the Parmesan cheese before serving.

SIDES

Calories: 110 • Fat: 8.5g • Protein: 3.5g • Total Carbs: 7g − Fiber: 4g = **Net Carbs: 3g**

PAN-FRIED CAULIFLOWER WITH SAGE

SIMPLY CARAMELIZED CAULIFLOWER FLORETS

"Caramelized cauliflower" has a nice ring to it, but it has an even better flavor! Whip up a side of these flavorful florets and you'll agree that, yes, George really knows how to cook with cauliflower.

SHOPPING LIST

1 small head cauliflower

1 tablespoon olive oil

2 tablespoons unsalted butter

¼ cup chicken broth or stock (may use water)

6 leaves sage, chopped

¼ teaspoon garlic powder

¼ teaspoon black pepper

2 tablespoons grated Parmesan cheese

Salt

HELPFUL TIPS

This same exact method can be used to cook 1 pound of asparagus, although they will only take 5–8 minutes to cook, and will only lightly brown before adding the chicken stock.

1 CUT cauliflower into small florets, discarding the large stem.

2 HEAT oil and butter in a large skillet over medium-high heat, until nearly smoking hot.

3 ADD the cauliflower florets to the hot skillet and toss to coat with oil and butter.

4 SAUTÉ, stirring only occasionally, until cauliflower is well browned, about 7 minutes.

5 ADD the chicken broth, sage, garlic powder, and pepper to the skillet and continue sautéing until most of the liquid has evaporated. The cauliflower should begin to brown once again and should now be crisp-tender.

6 REMOVE from heat and stir in Parmesan cheese. Season with salt to taste before serving.

SIDES

Calories: 115 • Fat: 10.5g • Protein: 3g • Total Carbs: 4g – Fiber: 2g = **Net Carbs: 2g**

LEEK GRATIN

TENDER GREEN ONIONS WITH CHEDDAR CHEESE

Some form of gratin is served in nearly every cuisine, with just about anything you can think of. Why? Because just about anything baked up like a casserole is going to taste amazing. This version incorporates a sorely overlooked vegetable: leeks. With a sweeter and more delicate flavor than its more famous cousins (onions and garlic), this gratin is a wonderful way for a sidelined star to finally step into the spotlight.

SHOPPING LIST

Nonstick cooking spray

2 pounds leeks, root ends trimmed, halved (see tip)

½ cup heavy cream

1 large egg white

½ teaspoon minced garlic

½ teaspoon salt

¼ teaspoon black pepper

1 cup shredded sharp Cheddar cheese

HELPFUL TIPS

To prep the leeks, you should first slice off about ½ inch of the bottom. Then you should remove 2–3 inches of the dark green tops, as they can be very tough and will not cook up as tender as the rest of the leek. After halving leeks, rinse well under running water to remove any grit from between leaves.

1 PREHEAT oven to 375°F. Spray an 8-inch square baking dish with nonstick cooking spray.

2 PLACE leeks in a single layer at the bottom of the prepared baking dish, slightly overlapping if there is not enough room.

3 IN a mixing bowl, whisk together the heavy cream, egg white, garlic, salt, and pepper. Pour evenly over the leeks in the baking dish.

4 SPRINKLE cheese over top of the leeks and sauce.

5 COVER with aluminum foil and bake for 30 minutes.

6 UNCOVER and bake an additional 8–10 minutes, or until leeks are tender and cheese is beginning to brown. Let cool for 5 minutes before serving.

SIDES

Calories: 185 • Fat: 10g • Protein: 7g • Total Carbs: 16.5g − Fiber: 2g = **Net Carbs: 14.5g**

BROILED ASPARAGUS

WITH ITALIAN VINAIGRETTE

Asparagus is too delicious to suffer a steamy fate in a basket above boiling water. Water simply doesn't add any flavor—but heat does—especially the high heat of your oven's broiler. Not only do the asparagus in this recipe get a nice tan under the broiler, they then take a delicious dip in a tangy Italian Vinaigrette.

SHOPPING LIST

1 pound asparagus, trimmed

1 tablespoon olive oil

ITALIAN VINAIGRETTE

2 tablespoons red wine vinegar

1 tablespoon extra virgin olive oil

½ teaspoon minced garlic

½ teaspoon Dijon mustard

½ teaspoon Italian seasoning

¼ teaspoon black pepper

⅛ teaspoon salt

HELPFUL TIPS

This recipe also works great with trimmed fresh green beans.

1 PLACE oven rack in the second highest position and heat broiler to high.

2 ON a sheet pan, toss asparagus in olive oil. Arrange in a single layer.

3 BROIL for 6–8 minutes, shaking the sheet pan halfway through to flip asparagus. Asparagus are done when somewhat charred, with stalks that are crisp-tender.

4 IN a small mixing bowl, whisk together all Italian Vinaigrette ingredients.

5 DRIZZLE the vinaigrette over the broiled asparagus and toss to coat before serving.

SIDES

Calories: 80 • Fat: 7g • Protein: 2g • Total Carbs: 3.5g – Fiber: 2g = **Net Carbs: 1.5g**

BRUSSELS SPROUTS WITH CRISPY PROSCIUTTO

PAN-ROASTED SPROUTS WITH CURED ITALIAN HAM

This buttery, pan-roasted, prosciutto-topped recipe is the perfect gateway preparation for Brussels sprouts skeptics. Eating your vegetables shouldn't feel like a chore, and just because these beautiful little cabbage bulbs are loaded with fiber, doesn't mean they can't also be loaded with delicious, crispy Italian ham.

SHOPPING LIST

2 tablespoons olive oil

1 tablespoon unsalted butter

1 pound Brussels sprouts, trimmed and halved

4 slices prosciutto, cut into strips

1 teaspoon minced garlic

1 teaspoon red wine vinegar

¼ teaspoon onion powder

¼ teaspoon black pepper

⅛ teaspoon salt

1 HEAT oil and butter in a large skillet over medium-high heat, until nearly smoking hot.

2 ADD the Brussels sprouts to the hot skillet. You should be able to hear them sizzling. Reduce heat to medium.

3 SAUTÉ sprouts until golden brown on both sides, about 7 minutes.

4 ADD all remaining ingredients to the skillet and sauté for an additional 2–3 minutes, just until prosciutto begins to crisp up. Serve immediately.

HELPFUL TIPS

Six strips of ordinary bacon can be used in place of the prosciutto by cooking in the skillet before preparing the rest of the dish. Remove from the skillet, crumble, and reserve until adding to the sprouts in step 4. You can also use the bacon grease that is left in the skillet to cook the sprouts (in place of the olive oil and butter).

SIDES

Calories: 115 • Fat: 8g • Protein: 5.5g • Total Carbs: 7g – Fiber: 2.5g = **Net Carbs: 4.5g**

DESSERTS

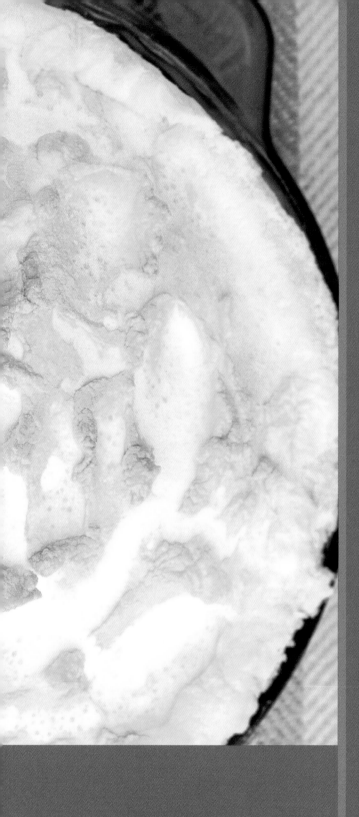

CONTENTS

PEANUT BUTTER COOKIE-CRUSTED CHEESECAKE

OUR FAMOUS NY CHEESECAKE WITH A NUTTY CRUST

Rachel and I have become more than a little famous for our low-carb New York cheesecake. Amazingly, we've never made a version of it with a true crust...until now!

SHOPPING LIST

Nonstick cooking spray

CRUST

1½ cups almond flour

4 tablespoons unsalted butter, melted, hot

1 large egg, beaten

3 tablespoons natural peanut butter

3 tablespoons sugar substitute

CAKE

24 ounces cream cheese, softened

1 cup ricotta cheese

1½ cups sugar substitute

⅓ cup heavy cream

2 large eggs

3 large egg yolks

1 tablespoon pure vanilla extract

1 tablespoon fresh lemon juice

CRUST DIRECTIONS

1 PLACE oven rack in center position. Preheat to 350°F. Spray an 8-inch springform pan with cooking spray.

2 IN a large bowl, combine the Crust ingredients, mixing well.

3 WHILE mixture is still warm from the butter, add it to the prepared pan. Use a piece of plastic wrap to press it evenly across the bottom. Discard the wrap.

4 BAKE Crust for 10–12 minutes, until lightly browned. Remove and let cool for 30 minutes.

CAKE DIRECTIONS

1 RAISE oven temperature to 400°F. Make a water bath by pouring 1 inch of hot water into a shallow roasting pan. Place the water bath onto the center rack to preheat.

2 WRAP the entire outside of the springform pan (with baked Crust) in aluminum foil to prevent any water from seeping into the cake.

3 WITH an electric mixer on low speed, beat the cream cheese, ricotta, and sugar substitute for about 1 minute, until well blended.

4 IN a separate bowl, whisk all remaining Cake ingredients, until blended.

5 TURN the mixer to medium speed and slowly pour the egg mixture into the cream cheese mixture. Beat just until all is blended.

6 POUR the batter over the crust in the pan and smooth out the top with a spatula. Place the pan in the heated water bath. Bake for 15 minutes.

7 LOWER the oven temperature to 325°F. Continue baking for 1½ hours, or until the top is a light golden brown and the cake is pulling away from the sides of the pan.

8 REMOVE from oven and let cool on counter for 1 hour. Cover and refrigerate for at least 8 hours before slicing to serve.

DESSERTS

Calories: 415 • Fat: 37g • Protein: 13g • Total Carbs: 9g – Fiber: 2g = **Net Carbs: 7g**

COCONUT CREAM BON BONS

A COCONUT CONFECTION TO CURB YOU SUGAR CRAVINGS

These pleasant bites remind me of a "Mounds" candy bar. If you add an almond on top of each bon bon after you coat them in chocolate, they will taste just like another "Joy"ful candy bar. Either way, you'll be jumping for "Joy" when you can have your candy and eat it, too!

SHOPPING LIST

4 ounces cream cheese

½ cup shredded unsweetened coconut

2 tablespoons sugar substitute

¼ teaspoon coconut extract

CHOCOLATE GANACHE

1 tablespoon unsalted butter

½ cup sugar substitute

2 teaspoons half-and-half

1 ounce unsweetened baking chocolate, chopped

1 teaspoon vanilla extract

HELPFUL TIPS

To add even more joy to your dessert, try pressing a whole almond into the tops of the coconut cream cheese balls before freezing.

1 LINE a small sheet pan or any freezer-safe dish with parchment paper.

2 IN a mixing bowl, use a fork to whisk together cream cheese, coconut, sugar substitute, and coconut extract.

3 FORM the mixture into 16 marble-sized balls. Place on the prepared sheet pan. Freeze for at least 30 minutes.

4 PREPARE the Chocolate Ganache following the directions below.

5 DIP the frozen cream cheese balls, one at a time, into the warm ganache, to coat. Work quickly before the chocolate cools. Place each coated bon bon back onto the parchment-lined dish.

6 FREEZE an additional 30 minutes, until the chocolate has hardened. Serve frozen, as these treats tend to melt in your hand.

Chocolate Ganache: Fill a pot with 2 inches of water and place over medium-high heat. Bring to a simmer and reduce temperature to low. Place a stainless steel bowl over the pot. Add the butter, sugar substitute, and half-and-half to the bowl and mix with a heat-proof spatula until combined. Add the chopped chocolate and stir just until melted. Remove from heat and stir in vanilla extract.

DESSERTS

Calories: 115 • Fat: 10g • Protein: 2g • Total Carbs: 4g – Fiber: 1g = **Net Carbs: 3g**

ALMOND CUPCAKES WITH MAPLE FROSTING

TOPPED WITH TOASTED ALMONDS

Almond flour, almond extract, AND toasted almonds, you ask? Yes, yes, and yes! When you realize cupcakes can taste this good, AND have ten grams of protein, you'll be wondering how to get even more almonds into them. But don't be almond-greedy. Save them. There are plenty of other recipes in this book you'll want to use them for.

SHOPPING LIST

CUPCAKES

Nonstick cooking spray

5 large eggs

¼ cup water

1 teaspoon almond extract

2½ cups blanched almond flour

¾ cup + 1 tablespoon sugar substitute

1 tablespoon baking powder

MAPLE FROSTING

¼ cup unsalted butter, softened

8 ounces cream cheese, softened

¾ cup sugar substitute

½ teaspoon maple extract

TOPPING

½ cup blanched almond slivers, toasted

Toasting almond slivers: Add the blanched almond slivers to a dry nonstick skillet over medium-high heat and shake the pan as they cook. Cook until lightly browned, only 2–3 minutes.

1 PLACE oven rack in the center position and preheat to 375°F. Line a 12-cup muffin pan with paper liners and spray each liner with nonstick cooking spray.

2 IN a large bowl, beat the eggs until frothy. Add the water and almond extract, and whisk to combine.

3 IN a separate bowl, mix the almond flour, sugar substitute, and baking powder.

4 BEAT the dry ingredients into the wet ingredients, until all is combined.

5 FILL the prepared muffin cups with an equal amount of the finished batter, filling each about ⅔ of the way full. (Using an ice cream scoop makes this easier.)

6 BAKE for 20–25 minutes, or until centers are firm and springy, and a toothpick inserted into a cupcake comes out mostly clean.

7 LET cool for 30 minutes before frosting each cupcake with the Maple Frosting and topping with toasted almond slivers. Store refrigerated.

Maple Frosting: Using an electric mixer, beat all Maple Frosting ingredients on high, until light and fluffy.

DESSERTS

Calories: 305 • Fat: 26.5g • Protein: 10g • Total Carbs: 10g – Fiber: 3g = **Net Carbs: 7g**

CRANBERRY PARFAITS

A LIGHT AND FLUFFY HOLIDAY DESSERT

Big holiday meals nearly always end with a big, heavy dessert…but sometimes the best desserts are the least conspicuous. The lightest. That refreshing last bite before you take that big holiday nap. These creamy parfaits swirled with a fresh cranberry compote are exactly what I'm talking about.

SHOPPING LIST

CRANBERRY COMPOTE

½ cup water

½ cup sugar substitute

6 ounces fresh or frozen cranberries

½ teaspoon orange zest

VANILLA CREAM

1 cup heavy cream

⅓ cup sugar substitute

1 teaspoon vanilla extract

½ teaspoon orange zest

HELPFUL TIPS

Be careful not to over-whip the cream in the electric mixer or it will get very thick and coat the roof of your mouth. That is the cream becoming butter!

1 PLACE all Cranberry Compote ingredients in a saucepan over medium-high heat.

2 BRING mixture to a boil, then reduce heat to a low simmer. Let simmer for about 7 minutes, stirring occasionally, until cranberries have split and begin to cook into a sauce.

3 LET Cranberry Compote cool for 30 minutes on counter. Cover and refrigerate at least 1 hour to fully chill before assembling the parfaits.

4 PREPARE the Vanilla Cream. With an electric mixer on high, whip the heavy cream, just until frothy.

5 ADD all remaining Vanilla Cream ingredients to the mixer. Whip on high speed until soft peaks form. Be careful not to over-whip.

6 PLACE a spoonful of the chilled Cranberry Compote in the bottom of each of 6 parfait glasses.

7 FOLD the remaining compote into the whipped Vanilla Cream, leaving visible streaks of red with peaks of white. Spoon over the compote in the parfait glasses and serve immediately. Can be refrigerated for up to 2 hours before serving.

DESSERTS

Calories: 100 • Fat: 7g • Protein: 0.5g • Total Carbs: 6.5g − Fiber: 1g = **Net Carbs: 5.5g**

MYLANO COOKIES

MY TAKE ON A FAVORITE SANDWICH COOKIE

Of all the reinventions I've made in this book, I must say that I am most proud of this one. Just have a look at them! If these don't look (and taste) identical to the cookies you'd buy in a store, then you must be good at not walking through that dastardly cookie aisle.

SHOPPING LIST

COOKIES

1 cup sugar substitute

2 ounces cream cheese, softened

2 tablespoons unsalted butter, softened

1 teaspoon vanilla extract

3 large egg whites

1 cup blanched almond flour

½ teaspoon baking soda

⅛ teaspoon salt

CHOCOLATE GANACHE

1 tablespoon unsalted butter

½ cup sugar substitute

2 teaspoons half-and-half

1 ounce unsweetened baking
    chocolate, chopped

1 teaspoon vanilla extract

Chocolate Ganache: Fill a pot with 2 inches of water and place over medium-high heat. Bring to a simmer and reduce temperature to low. Place a stainless steel bowl over the pot. Add the butter, sugar substitute, and half-and-half to the bowl and mix with a heat-proof spatula until combined. Add the chopped chocolate and stir just until melted. Remove from heat and stir in the vanilla extract.

1 PREHEAT oven to 350°F. Line a sheet pan with parchment paper.

2 ADD the sugar substitute, cream cheese, butter, and vanilla extract to an electric mixer set to low. Mix until blended. Raise the speed to high and continue mixing until creamy.

3 TURN the mixer back down to low and slowly add the egg whites.

4 GRADUALLY add the almond flour, baking soda, and salt, and mix until just combined. Be careful not to over-mix.

5 ADD dough to a pastry bag with an open tip or a gallon freezer bag with the corner cut off. Pipe 2-inch long cookies onto the lined pan, leaving a couple of inches between each. You should have enough dough to pipe 20 cookies. Lift and gently tap the pan on the counter to slightly flatten the cookies.

6 BAKE for 10–12 minutes, until edges of cookies are lightly browned. Let cool completely.

7 PREPARE the Chocolate Ganache (directions on left).

8 SPREAD a thin layer of warm chocolate ganache between 2 cooled cookies to make a sandwich. Repeat with all remaining cookies. Refrigerate at least 30 minutes before serving.

DESSERTS

Calories: 150 • Fat: 12g • Protein: 4g • Total Carbs: 7g − Fiber: 2g = **Net Carbs: 5g**

TOASTED HAZELNUT CHOCOLATE CUPCAKES

IT'S GOT DOUBLE THE CHOCOLATE AND DOUBLE THE HAZELNUT

These cupcakes have the flavors of chocolate and hazelnut baked throughout, but that wasn't enough for me.... I've also topped them with Chocolate Ganache and toasted hazelnuts for a double dose of delicious decadence.

SHOPPING LIST

Nonstick cooking spray

4 large eggs

2 large egg whites

2 tablespoons unsalted butter, melted

¼ cup water

1 teaspoon hazelnut extract

2½ cups almond flour

1 cup sugar substitute

¼ cup unsweetened cocoa powder

1 tablespoon baking powder

¾ cup hazelnuts, coarsely chopped

CHOCOLATE GANACHE

2 tablespoons unsalted butter

1 cup sugar substitute

4 teaspoons half-and-half

2 ounces unsweetened baking chocolate, chopped

2 teaspoons vanilla extract

1 PLACE oven rack in the center position and preheat to 375°F. Spray a 12-cup muffin pan with nonstick cooking spray.

2 IN a large mixing bowl, beat the eggs and egg whites until frothy. Whisk in melted butter, water, and hazelnut extract, until combined.

3 IN a separate bowl, mix the almond flour, sugar substitute, cocoa powder, and baking powder.

4 WHISK the dry ingredients into the wet ingredients, until all is combined.

5 FILL the prepared muffin cups with an equal amount of the finished batter, filling each about ⅔ of the way full.

6 BAKE for 20–25 minutes, or until cupcakes are spongy, and a toothpick inserted into the center of one comes out mostly clean. Let cool completely.

7 TOAST the chopped hazelnuts in a dry nonstick skillet over medium heat for 3 minutes, or until lightly browned.

8 FROST each cupcake with a thin layer of warm Chocolate Ganache (see directions below). Press the toasted hazelnuts into the ganache. Serve chilled for best flavor.

Chocolate Ganache: Fill a pot with 2 inches of water and place over medium-high heat. Bring to a simmer and reduce temperature to low. Place a stainless steel bowl over the pot. Add the butter, sugar substitute, and half-and-half to the bowl and mix with a heat-proof spatula until combined. Add the chopped chocolate and stir just until melted. Remove from heat and stir in the vanilla extract.

DESSERTS

Calories: 280 • Fat: 22.5g • Protein: 9.5g • Total Carbs: 13g – Fiber: 4.5g = **Net Carbs: 8.5g**

COCONUT POUND CAKE

WITH COCONUT CREAM CHEESE FROSTING

Bring the taste of the tropics into your house with this nutty twist on a classic (low-carb) pound cake...coconutty twist that is! With coconut in the cake AND the frosting, you've got almost no choice but to sit back, relax, and soak up the island lifestyle.

SHOPPING LIST

Nonstick cooking spray

2½ cups blanched almond flour

1½ cups sugar substitute

1½ teaspoons baking powder

½ teaspoon salt

¾ cup unsalted butter, softened

6 ounces cream cheese, softened

7 large eggs, beaten

2 teaspoons coconut extract

1½ teaspoons fresh lemon juice

FROSTING

4 ounces cream cheese, softened

⅓ cup sugar substitute

2 tablespoons unsalted butter, softened

¼ teaspoon coconut extract

TOPPING (OPTIONAL)

¼ cup unsweetened shredded coconut

HELPFUL TIPS

Unsweetened shredded coconut can be hard to find. You can grate your own from fresh coconut, but we've found that they sell it in the baking aisle of Wal-Mart (but not our local grocery store).

1 PLACE oven rack in center position and preheat to 375°F. Line a 9x5-inch loaf pan with parchment paper and spray paper with nonstick cooking spray.

2 IN a mixing bowl, combine the almond flour, sugar substitute, baking powder, and salt.

3 WITH an electric mixer on high speed, beat the butter and cream cheese until mixed. Add the beaten eggs, coconut extract, and lemon juice, and beat until smooth.

4 SLOWLY fold the dry ingredients into the wet ingredients until a batter is formed.

5 POUR the batter into the prepared loaf pan and smooth out the top. Bake for 1 hour, or until the top begins to brown and a toothpick inserted into the center comes out mostly clean. Let cool for at least 10 minutes before removing from the pan. Let cool completely.

6 PREPARE the Coconut Cream Cheese Frosting by adding all Frosting ingredients to a clean electric mixer. Beat on high until light and fluffy.

7 SPREAD frosting onto the pound cake and sprinkle with unsweetened coconut, if desired. Let chill for at least 2 hours before slicing into 6 thick slices and then cutting each slice in half to make 12 portions. Store refrigerated.

DESSERTS

Calories: 405 • Fat: 37g • Protein: 10.5g • Total Carbs: 10g − Fiber: 3g = **Net Carbs: 7g**

KEY LIME PANNA COTTA

KEY WEST - MEETS ITALY - MEETS GEORGE

This Italian classic gets a jolt of Key West zest in an inspired mash-up of flavors from my heritage, and my adopted home state. Florida and Italy. Italy and Florida. The sweet, succulent flavors in this dessert will tug you in both directions. Just make sure you don't end up in the middle. The Bermuda Triangle is out there somewhere.

SHOPPING LIST

Nonstick cooking spray

4 large eggs

1 cup half-and-half

4 ounces cream cheese, softened

½ cup sugar substitute

¼ cup Key lime juice

2 teaspoons minced Key
    lime zest (see tip)

1 teaspoon vanilla extract

HELPFUL TIPS

Regular lime zest can be used in place of the Key lime zest, however it is definitely recommended that you use true Key lime juice. Most stores sell Key lime juice in bottles in either the baking aisle or produce section.

1 ADD 1 inch of water to a shallow roasting pan to make a water bath. Place on the center oven rack before preheating oven to 350°F.

2 SPRAY 6 small custard cups (ramekins) with nonstick cooking spray.

3 ADD eggs to a large mixing bowl or electric mixer and beat until frothy.

4 ADD all remaining ingredients to the bowl and beat until well combined.

5 POUR equal amounts of the mixture into the 6 prepared custard cups.

6 CAREFULLY place the filled custard cups directly into the preheated water bath. Bake for 45–50 minutes, or until a toothpick inserted into the center comes out mostly clean.

7 LET cool on counter for 1 hour. Cover and refrigerate for an additional 3 hours before serving. Run a thin knife around the custard and invert the cup onto the serving plate to release.

DESSERTS

Calories: 180 • Fat: 14.5g • Protein: 7g • Total Carbs: 4.5g − Fiber: 0g = **Net Carbs: 4.5g**

PUMPKIN SPICE MINUTE MUFFIN

WITH EGGNOG FROSTING

I hope you aren't allergic to adorable desserts, because if so, you'll want to avoid this amazing, one-minute-muffin in a mug. Thankfully, I don't believe such an allergy to the adorable exists, so feel free to whip these up for the whole family. They are absolutely delicious, and insanely quick to make.

SHOPPING LIST

MUFFIN

¼ cup almond flour

1 large egg

1 tablespoon ground flax seed (golden is best)

2 tablespoons sugar substitute

1 teaspoon unsalted butter, melted

½ teaspoon baking powder

½ teaspoon pumpkin pie spice

EGGNOG FROSTING

1 ounce cream cheese

1 teaspoon unsalted butter, softened

1 tablespoon sugar substitute

⅛ teaspoon vanilla extract

1 pinch nutmeg

1 ADD all Muffin ingredients to a microwave-safe mug.

2 WHISK with a fork until all ingredients are well combined.

3 MICROWAVE for 1 minute on high, or until the batter rises in the mug and a toothpick inserted into the center comes out mostly clean.

4 IN a small bowl, whisk all Eggnog Frosting ingredients with a fork. Spread over the cooked muffin before serving.

HELPFUL TIPS

If the muffin is not entirely set, only cook for an additional 5–10 seconds at a time. These things cook fast! One minute always works perfect for us.

DESSERTS

Calories: 450 • Fat: 39g • Protein: 16.5g • Total Carbs: 11.5g – Fiber: 5.5g = **Net Carbs: 6g**

FROZEN PECAN DELIGHT BITES

JUST LIKE PECAN NOUGAT LOGS

Patience is a virtue with these fluffy, frozen pecan delights. Making them is incredibly simple. Waiting for them to set in the freezer is going to be incredibly difficult. But you can do it. I believe in you. Maybe flip through this book and find something to try for dinner tomorrow. Or…just stare at the freezer door for two hours. It's okay; I understand. They're THAT good.

SHOPPING LIST

6 ounces cream cheese, softened

2 tablespoons unsalted butter, softened

⅓ cup sugar substitute

1 teaspoon vanilla extract

¼ cup chopped pecans

HELPFUL TIPS

Any type of roasted nut will work in this recipe. Roasted hazelnuts or pistachios are particularly good.

1 LINE a small sheet pan (or any container that will fit in your freezer) with parchment paper.

2 PLACE cream cheese, butter, sugar substitute, and vanilla extract in an electric mixer.

3 SET mixer to high and mix until ingredients are light and fluffy.

4 FOLD the chopped pecans into the beaten cream cheese mixture.

5 DROP tablespoons of the mixture onto the parchment paper until all is used up. You should get about 16 pieces.

6 COVER and freeze for 2 hours before serving.

DESSERTS

Calories: 130 • Fat: 13g • Protein: 2g • Total Carbs: 2g – Fiber: 0g = **Net Carbs: 2g**

UPSIDE DOWN BERRY CRISP PIE

WITH OR WITHOUT FAUX VANILLA ICE CREAM

We love to use an assortment of fresh berries in this pie that is literally all-mixed-up. With a crust on the top, I'd suppose this is technically a "crisp" or "cobbler," but it all tastes like pie to me! Though it is entirely optional, the Faux Vanilla Ice Cream is already included in the nutritional information at the bottom of this recipe.

SHOPPING LIST

Nonstick cooking spray

2 cups any mixed berries, fresh or frozen

1/3 cup sugar substitute

1/2 cup chopped walnuts

CRUST

1 large egg

1/2 cup sugar substitute

1/2 cup almond flour

FAUX VANILLA ICE CREAM

1 cup heavy cream

1/2 cup sugar substitute

2 tablespoons whole milk ricotta cheese

1 teaspoon no-suga-added vanilla extract

HELPFUL TIPS

Leftovers taste best when reheated. Bake at 325°F for 15 minutes, or until warmed throughout.

1 PREHEAT oven to 325°F. Spray a 10-inch deep-dish pie pan with nonstick cooking spray.

2 PLACE the berries into the pie pan and sprinkle with the first measure of sugar substitute. Top with the chopped walnuts.

3 CREATE the Crust by adding the egg and sugar substitute to a mixing bowl, and whisking until frothy. Using a rubber spatula, fold the almond flour into the egg mixture.

4 POUR the Crust mixture over the berries, using a spatula to spread the mixture out to about 1/2 inch away from the edge of the pie pan.

5 BAKE for 40–45 minutes, or until top is golden brown.

6 REMOVE and let cool for 5 minutes before serving. Serve warm topped with a scoop of Faux Vanilla Ice Cream, if desired.

Faux Vanilla Ice Cream: Using an electric mixer, beat all ingredients until soft peaks form. Cover and freeze for at least 1 hour before scooping as you would ordinary ice cream.

DESSERTS

Calories: 185 • Fat: 15g • Protein: 4.5g • Total Carbs: 10.5g − Fiber: 2.5g = **Net Carbs: 8g**

PUMPKIN MERINGUE PIE

WE MERGE TWO FAMOUS PIES FOR ONE PERFECT RESULT

Pumpkin pie is a standard for us around the holidays and we've made it all sorts of ways. This is the first time that we've made it with a truly crunchy crust that doesn't compromise. This is also the first time that we've topped it with fluffy, marshmallow-y meringue. It just doesn't get any more perfect than this!

SHOPPING LIST

Nonstick cooking spray

CRUST

2 cups blanched almond flour

¼ cup sugar substitute

2 tablespoons unsalted butter, softened

1 large egg

FILLING

1 (15-ounce) can pure pumpkin

1¼ cups heavy cream

4 large eggs, beaten

¾ cup sugar substitute

1 tablespoon pumpkin pie spice

MERINGUE

4 large egg whites, room temperature

¼ cup sugar substitute

½ teaspoon vanilla extract

¼ teaspoon cream of tartar

HELPFUL TIPS

You can also skip the Meringue in this recipe for a standard Pumpkin Pie. Simply bake for 30 minutes in step 7, or until filling jiggles, but is mostly set. Chill at least 2 hours.

1 PLACE oven rack in the center position and preheat to 350°F. Spray a 10-inch deep-dish pie pan with nonstick cooking spray.

2 PLACE all Crust ingredients in a food processor and pulse until a dough is formed.

3 PLACE dough into the prepared pie pan. Cover with plastic wrap and press down to spread the dough evenly across the bottom and up the sides of the pan. Discard plastic wrap.

4 BAKE Crust for 10–12 minutes, or until lightly browned. Let cool as you make the Filling.

5 TURN the oven up to 425°F.

6 IN a large mixing bowl, whisk together all Filling ingredients, until fully combined. Pour into the baked Crust.

7 BAKE for 15 minutes at 425°F. Reduce heat to 350°F and bake an additional 25 minutes.

8 MEANWHILE, make the Meringue. Add the egg whites to an electric mixer. Beat on high until frothy. Add all remaining Meringue ingredients and continue beating on high until stiff peaks form. Spread the Meringue over the baked pie, mounding it up high.

9 BAKE a final 15 minutes, or until Meringue is lightly browned. Cool on the counter for 1 hour. Chill for at least 3 hours before slicing to serve.

DESSERTS

Calories: 225 • Fat: 18g • Protein: 9g • Total Carbs: 9g – Fiber: 3.5g = **Net Carbs: 5.5g**

BLUEBERRY CHEESECAKE MOUSSE

DECADENT FRUIT-ON-THE-BOTTOM PARFAITS

From the French meaning "perfect," parfait sure thinks highly of itself.... But with good reason! It's cool, sweet, smooth, and even easy on the eyes. Especially this variation, which is swirled with violet streaks of mouthwatering, fresh blueberry purée. It's like a succulent, edible galaxy of fruit and cream.

SHOPPING LIST

2 cups blueberries, plus additional for garnish

⅓ cup + 2 tablespoons sugar substitute, divided

1 cup heavy cream

1½ teaspoons vanilla extract

½ teaspoon lemon zest

8 ounces cream cheese, softened

Fresh mint, for garnish

HELPFUL TIPS

Fresh or frozen blueberries can be used in this recipe, though frozen blueberries should be thawed before blending.

1 USING a blender or food processor, purée blueberries with the 2 tablespoons of sugar substitute, blending until smooth. Set aside.

2 WITH an electric mixer on high, whip the heavy cream, just until frothy.

3 ADD the ⅓ cup of sugar substitute, vanilla extract, lemon zest, and softened cream cheese to the mixer and whip on high speed, just until soft peaks form. Be careful not to over-whip.

4 USE a spatula to fold ¼ of the blueberry purée into the cheesecake mousse, leaving visible streaks of blue and white.

5 SPOON an equal amount of the remaining ¾ of blueberry purée into the bottom of 6 parfait glasses. Top each with the swirled cheesecake mousse and serve chilled. Garnish with fresh blueberries and mint, if desired.

Calories: 240 • Fat: 21g • Protein: 3.5g • Total Carbs: 10.5g − Fiber: 1g = **Net Carbs: 9.5g**

RED VELVET COOKIES

IF YOU LIKE THE CAKE, YOU'RE GONNA LOVE THE COOKIE

A decadent American favorite for more than seventy-five years, the red velvet cake has an air of sophistication and indulgence about it. Here, I respectfully tweak the time-honored tradition and turn a classic cake into cookies without losing any of the flavor, or that beloved, dark red color. So go ahead…indulge.

SHOPPING LIST

2 ounces cream cheese, softened

2 tablespoons unsalted butter, softened

1 cup sugar substitute

1 large egg

1 teaspoon vanilla extract

1 cup blanched almond flour

1 tablespoon unsweetened cocoa powder

½ teaspoon baking soda

6 drops red food coloring

HELPFUL TIPS

The red food coloring is technically not needed to make these cookies, but they won't look anything like "red" velvet without it.

1 PREHEAT oven to 375°F. Line a sheet pan with parchment paper.

2 ADD the cream cheese, butter, sugar substitute, egg, and vanilla extract to an electric mixer. Set to high and mix until creamy and fluffy.

3 ADD all remaining ingredients and mix on medium until well blended.

4 USING a tablespoon or 1-ounce ice cream scoop, drop 16 evenly spaced cookies onto the prepared sheet pan. Lightly tap the pan on the counter to flatten cookies.

5 BAKE for 8–10 minutes, just until the centers have set. Let cool for 10 minutes before serving.

DESSERTS

Calories: 155 • Fat: 13g • Protein: 4.5g • Total Carbs: 6.5g – Fiber: 1.5g = **Net Carbs: 5g**

ITALIAN WHIPPED CREAM FROSTING

LIGHT AND FLUFFY VANILLA FROSTING WITH A HINT OF ALMOND

This sweet, airy cream frosting has the subtle flavor of an Italian amaretto. It tastes great on almost anything. Try a dollop in your coffee. Or, better still, remember that red velvet cookie recipe (page 214)? I'm just saying that you should definitely put this frosting on those cookies. I'm just saying.

SHOPPING LIST

2 cups heavy whipping cream

½ cup ricotta cheese

½ cup sugar substitute

1 teaspoon vanilla extract

¼ teaspoon almond extract

HELPFUL TIPS

In a pinch, ½ teaspoon of additional vanilla extract can be used in place of the almond extract, however this is truly best when made as written…but of course I would say that, seeing as it is my recipe!

1 WITH an electric mixer on high, whip the heavy cream, just until frothy.

2 ADD the ricotta cheese, sugar substitute, vanilla extract, and almond extract to the heavy cream.

3 SET the mixer to low speed and mix until all ingredients are incorporated.

4 SET the mixer to high speed and continue whipping until soft peaks form.

5 COVER and refrigerate until ready to use. Store baked goods frosted with this frosting for up to 4 days in the refrigerator.

DESSERTS

Calories: 90 • Fat: 8g • Protein: 1.5g • Total Carbs: 2g – Fiber: 0g = **Net Carbs: 2g**

ICE CREAM SANDWICHES

CHOCOLATE COOKIES WITH FAUX VANILLA ICE CREAM FILLING

These faux ice cream sandwiches are an amazing low-carb concoction, if I do say so myself. You could smoosh these fresh-baked chocolate cookies on either side of anything and it would be delicious, but luckily, you don't need to use just anything. The mock vanilla ice cream in the middle of these sandwiches will convince you that "faux" is not a four-letter word.

SHOPPING LIST

COOKIES

2 ounces cream cheese, softened

2 tablespoons unsalted butter, softened

1 large egg

¾ cup sugar substitute

1 teaspoon vanilla extract

1 cup almond flour

1 tablespoon unsweetened cocoa powder

½ teaspoon baking soda

FILLING

½ cup heavy cream

¼ cup sugar substitute

1½ tablespoons ricotta cheese

½ teaspoon vanilla extract

2 drops almond extract

HELPFUL TIPS

Use a pastry bag to pipe the filling onto the cookies for a more even and clean presentation.

1 PREHEAT oven to 350°F. Line a sheet pan with parchment paper.

2 PLACE cream cheese, butter, egg, sugar substitute, and vanilla extract in an electric mixer. Beat on high until smooth and fluffy.

3 ADD the almond flour, cocoa powder, and baking soda to the mixture in the mixer. Beat on medium, just until combined into a thin dough.

4 USING a tablespoon or 1-ounce ice cream scoop, drop 12 evenly spaced dollops of the dough onto the prepared sheet pan. Cover the dollops with plastic wrap and press down lightly, to flatten. Discard plastic wrap.

5 BAKE for 8–10 minutes, just until Cookies are springy in the center. Let cool for at least 20 minutes.

6 MEANWHILE, prepare the Filling by adding all ingredients to a clean electric mixer. Beat until light and fluffy.

7 SPREAD a thick layer of the Filling in between 2 cooled Cookies. Repeat until you've made 6 sandwiches.

8 COVER and freeze for at least 4 hours before serving.

DESSERTS

Calories: 245 • Fat: 21g • Protein: 6.5g • Total Carbs: 9g − Fiber: 2g = **Net Carbs: 7g**

STRAWBERRY DELIGHT LAYER CAKE

THERE'S NOTHING SHORT ABOUT THIS FULL-SIZED CAKE

This stunning strawberry layer cake is like a giant shortcake with plenty to serve a room full of guests. Piled high with my Italian Whipped Cream Frosting and oodles of fresh strawberries, this one's a real beauty that would be a shame to eat.... But you will definitely eat it.

SHOPPING LIST

Nonstick cooking spray

¾ cup + 1 tablespoon sugar substitute

5 large eggs

¼ cup water

1 tablespoon vanilla extract

2½ cups blanched almond flour

1 tablespoon baking powder

1 batch Italian Whipped Cream
    Frosting, recipe page: 215

2 cups sliced fresh strawberries

Note: The nutritional information below already includes the Italian Whipped Cream Frosting.

1 PLACE oven rack in center position and preheat to 350°F. Spray an 8-inch round cake pan with nonstick cooking spray. Sprinkle the 1 tablespoon of sugar substitute around the bottom and edges of the greased pan.

2 IN a large mixing bowl, beat the eggs, water, and vanilla extract, until frothy.

3 In a separate mixing bowl, combine almond flour, baking powder, and the ¾ cup sugar substitute.

4 Whisk the dry ingredients into the wet ingredients until a batter is formed. Pour the batter into the prepared cake pan and smooth out the top.

5 BAKE for 30–35 minutes, or until the center is springy, and a toothpick inserted into it comes out mostly clean. Let cool for at least 10 minutes before removing from the pan.

6 LET cool on counter for 30 minutes. Cover and refrigerate for at least 2 hours.

7 INVERT pan onto a large plate and shake to release cake. Using a bread knife, carefully slice the entire cake into 2 layers horizontally. Place the bottom layer on a serving dish.

8 FROST the top of the bottom layer with the Italian Whipped Cream Frosting. Place a single layer of sliced strawberries over top of the frosting.

9 TOP with the second layer of cake. Frost the top and all sides of the cake with the frosting. Arrange the remaining sliced strawberries over top of the frosted cake. Refrigerate for an additional 2 hours before slicing to serve.

DESSERTS

Calories: 265 • Fat: 22g • Protein: 9.5g • Total Carbs: 10g — Fiber: 3g = **Net Carbs: 7g**

RECIPE INDEX

BREAKFAST

LUNCH

RECIPE INDEX

MEATS

SEAFOOD

SIDE DISHES

DESSERTS

ABOUT THE AUTHOR

George Stella has been a professional chef for over 30 years. He has appeared on numerous television and news shows, including two seasons of his own show, *Low Carb and Lovin' It*, on the Food Network. Most recently he appeared on *The Dr. Oz Show* for a profile on the comfort foods the Stella family reinvented using unique and low-carb alternatives to white flour and sugar.

Connecticut born, George has spent more than half of his life in Florida, where he lives today, with his wife Rachel. This is his seventh cookbook.

To keep up to date on George, please visit:

www.StellaStyle.com

ABOUT THE PHOTOGRAPHY

The food photographs and design of this book were done by **Christian and Elise Stella**, George's son and daughter-in-law. They have worked previously on the design and photography of eighteen cookbooks for various authors. They are frequent collaborators with Bob Warden and did the design, photography, and co-authored his bestselling cookbook *Great Food Fast*.

All food in the photographs was purchased at an ordinary grocery store or grown in Rachel's garden. It was prepared to the recipe's directions. No artificial food styling techniques were used to "enhance" the food's appearance.